# KNOWING WHAT THE LAW IS

This book provides a selective and somewhat cheeky account of prominent positions in legal theory, such as American legal realism, modern legal positivism, sociological systems theory, institutionalism and critical legal studies. It presents a relational approach to law and a new perspective on legal sources.

The book explores topics of legal theory in a playful manner. It is written and composed in a way that refutes the widespread prejudice that legal theory is a dreary subject, with a cast of characters that occasionally interact in order to illustrate the claims of the book.

Legal experts claim to know what the law is. Legal theory – or jurisprudence – explores whether such claims are warranted. The discipline first emerged at the turn of the 20th century, when the self-confidence of both legal scholarship and judicial craftsmanship became severely shattered, but the crisis continues to this day.

# KNOWING WHAT THE LAW IS

## Legal Theory in a New Key

*Alexander Somek*

· H A R T ·

OXFORD · LONDON · NEW YORK · NEW DELHI · SYDNEY

HART PUBLISHING

Bloomsbury Publishing Plc

Kemp House, Chawley Park, Cumnor Hill, Oxford, OX2 9PH, UK

1385 Broadway, New York, NY 10018, USA

29 Earlsfort Terrace, Dublin 2, Ireland

HART PUBLISHING, the Hart/Stag logo, BLOOMSBURY and the Diana logo are
trademarks of Bloomsbury Publishing Plc

First published in Great Britain 2021

Cover painting: *Blind Date* by Xenia Hausner

A catalogue record for this book is available from the British Library.

Library of Congress Cataloging-in-Publication data

Names: Somek, Alexander, 1961- author.

Title: Knowing what the law is : legal theory in a new key / Alexander Somek.

Other titles: Rechtstheorie zur Einführung. English

Description: Oxford ; New York : Hart, 2021. | Includes bibliographical references and index.

Identifiers: LCCN 2021021412 (print) | LCCN 2021021413 (ebook) |
ISBN 9781509951291 (hardback) | ISBN 9781509951338 (paperback) |
ISBN 9781509951314 (pdf) | ISBN 9781509951307 (Epub)

Subjects: LCSH: Law—Philosophy.

Classification: LCC K230.S649 A3713 2021 (print) | LCC K230.S649 (ebook) | DDC 340/.1—dc23

LC record available at https://lccn.loc.gov/2021021412

LC ebook record available at https://lccn.loc.gov/2021021413

ISBN:  HB:     978-1-50995-129-1
       ePDF:   978-1-50995-131-4
       ePub:   978-1-50995-130-7

Typeset by Compuscript Ltd, Shannon

To find out more about our authors and books visit www.hartpublishing.co.uk. Here you will find
extracts, author information, details of forthcoming events and the option to sign up for our newsletters.

# *Preface*

This book was written in an attempt to communicate to both the uninitiated and the initiated that legal theory is a highly enjoyable ('fun') field of study. Alas, the discipline has suffered drawbacks over the last few decades as the intellectual excitement that it offers has often been eclipsed by pedantry. This is what happens when disciplines become dominated by schools or major hubs. They attract 'followers' whose work is then mostly scholastic and, hence, absorbed in pseudo-problems.

This work is short and far from comprehensive. I regret that ideas of some of the most ingenious scholars had to be left out, both for reasons of brevity and for a lack of fit with the story that I am trying to tell in this book. The story can be read as an introduction to legal theory, which I complement with glimpses of my own approach. It is meant to explain why I am taking this route.

A less extensive and elaborate predecessor version of this text appeared in German in 2017. I would like to thank Steffen Herrmann of Junius Verlag for allowing me to go forward and to publish this considerably revised and amended version in English. It had its origin in introductory courses that I have taught at the University of Iowa and the University of Vienna over the course of the last 17 years.

The English version of the manuscript was read by my dear friend and former colleague Todd Pettys and by Paul Menke, who was enrolled in the latest jurisprudence class that I taught at Iowa in 2020. I would like to thank both for their thoughtful comments and Todd, in particular, for generously taking out time to read this rather special work.

Urszula Kosielińska-Grabowska was kind enough to share her expertise on Scandinavian realism with me.

The work has benefited from the diligence with which Astrid Mayer and Hanna Mosler went about editing the text and the footnotes. Franziska Eckstein helped with the bibliography.

I am deeply indebted to Xenia Hausner for granting me permission to use her painting *Blind Date* as a jacket illustration. It is comforting to know that at least in one respect the book bears the mark of genius.

Finally, I would like to thank Kate Whetter of Hart Publishing for the steadfast enthusiasm with which she supported this rather unconventional project.

Alexander Somek                                    Vienna, February 2021

# Contents

# Legal Knowledge

## § 1

Legal theory explores the conditions under which legal knowledge is possible. Knowledge of this kind claims to know what is right or wrong, legally speaking.

It is no small task to reassure oneself of its possibility. After all, the law only exists because some have successfully claimed to know what the law is. Without any such knowledge, there would be no law.

## § 2

Being known, hence, is not external to the law.

> *Object (to the viewer)*: I give a damn on whether you know me or not.

> *Viewer (to the object, with arms crossed)*: Oh, shut up, object, you don't talk.

It is not the case that there is, on one side, the law and, on the other, knowledge of it, as though there was no internal connection between them, but only a relation of external reference. On the contrary, the validity of legal rules and the existence of legal institutions (such as contracts) are based upon knowledge claims.

Any contract that wants to be something, legally speaking, comes to this world with an implicit reflexive statement concerning its own binding character.[1] It knows about its own being as a contract or at least *believes* to know this fact.

> *Contract*: Hi there, I'm not just a piece of prose.

When the legislature becomes active, it implicitly presupposes the truth of the statement according to which it has been given the power to legislate.

Any raising of a legal claim is mediated by legal knowledge.

This mediation is not a one-way street. It runs in two directions.

---

[1] The following sections of this chapter echo ideas to be found in Hans Kelsen's *Introduction to the Problems of Legal Theory* (trans B Litschewski Paulson and SL Paulson, Oxford, Clarendon Press, 1992) 1–5. This theme has been taken up recently by Christoph Kletzer in his *The Idea of a Pure Theory of Law* (Oxford, Hart Publishing, 2018) 79–90.

## § 3

One direction leads from legal knowledge to law:

*Mother*:  You mustn't do that; it would upset other people.

*Child*: I mustn't?

*Mother*: No.

The knowledge that there is a rule prohibiting conduct and that certain behaviours would be transgressions of this rule provides insight into what is legally forbidden.

## § 4

The mediation, however, also runs in the other direction:

*Party*: This contract violates the order of creation.

*Judge*: So what?

What purports to be legal knowledge is socially relevant only insofar as it is not rejected as irrelevant or outlandish by those mastering the practice of knowing the law. Much aspires to be legal knowledge that does not reach the threshold of relevance. In any case, it is not admitted to the game of making legal statements if it fails to convey that it originates from trained legal thinking (from 'thinking like a lawyer' as we say in the USA[2]).

> *Party*: Contracts that violate the order of creation offend public morals and are therefore void.

> *Judge*: Where do you derive that from?

> *Party*: Well, from *lex naturalis*, of course. It is the imprint that the eternal divine law – the *lex aeterna* – has left in the human soul – like a signet ring, you know *(presses the fist of one hand against the palm of the other for purposes of demonstration)*.[3]

> *The judge clears her throat and somewhat embarrassedly skims through the file. She then turns to opposing counsel*: Shall we continue?

---

[2] For a highly elaborate introduction, see F Schauer, *Thinking like a Lawyer* (Cambridge, MA, Harvard University Press, 2009).

[3] The talk of the *lex aeterna* as being stamped into the human soul as *lex naturalis* alludes to Augustine, *De Trinitate* XIV 15 21, http://www.logoslibrary.org/augustine/trinity/1415.html. Augustine, *On the Trinity: Books 8–15* (trans S McKenna, Cambridge, Cambridge University Press, 2002) XIV 15 21, p 160.

In order to be what it aspires to be, any presentation of knowledge of the law, regardless of whether it is bound to remain controversial, must garner recognition by those who practise law, at least when it comes to observing conventions of presentation.

*Counsel (hissing at the party)*: You don't say such a thing here!

The relevant threshold of recognition shows that, practically speaking, the law is not only the object, but also the subject of its knowledge. Law is not only a bunch of norms. To the law belongs also the thinking apprehension of norms. The law possesses subjectivity and objectivity.

Legal knowledge is a form of self-knowledge. It is knowledge of the law by the law.

*Pupil*: I am not sure I understood this.

*Thinker*: Neither am I. But let's see how this continues.

## § 5

In the shape that it is given within legal scholarship, legal knowledge is tailored to provide reasons for a court decision or an act of the administration. Ultimately, such acts are meant to distinguish right from wrong. They do so by deciding on a legal claim. Legal knowledge determines what one person owes to another or what is a person's due.

Recast within the format of legal scholarship, general legal norms are rendered in a manner that makes them suitable for asserting and assessing individual legal claims. On the 'sibylline leaves' of official decisions we discover how the law comes to apprehend itself.[4]

The reasons supporting decisions are embodiments of legal knowledge in *legally* relevant form.

## § 6

The subjectivity of law is manifest above all in how the law is practised. Activity is something that is going on in this world. Legal knowledge – the subjective dimension of law – is, therefore, objective in a sense that says

---

[4] The 'sibylline leaves' are an allusion to Oliver Wendell Holmes' reference to the sibylline leaves of law reports in his 'The Path of the Law' (1897) 10 *Harvard Law Review* 457–78, 457.

nothing about its potential accuracy with regard to what the law is. Practices of legal knowledge, which are more often than not informed by scholarly training, are social facts lending expression to intellectual habits.

> *Initiate*: That's how you argue in civil law.

> *Judge*: A criminal law problem is approached as follows …

Habitual legal knowledge is not merely a web of ideas. It exists in a social space. It is objective in a sociological sense. There are legal experts who provide companies and institutions with their services. No small part of these services is to impart legal knowledge.

> *Thinker*: The thinking subject is part of the world of objects. In this respect, its thinking is objective.

Objectivity in such a sociological sense needs to be distinguished from the critical claim to objectivity inherent in legal knowledge. This is the claim to provide an objective – ie non-perspectival, unbiased, neutral and subjectively untainted – account of the law. This critical dimension is implicit in any claim to know what the law is. In raising a knowledge claim, every expertise invariably embraces objectivity in a critical sense and, hence, must be ready to elaborate, if challenged, what it is that accounts for the truth of that claim.[5]

Without losing its quality of being a claim to knowledge, an expert statement cannot admit cynically that it is merely a means of fooling, deceiving or cheating an opponent. For it is the observance of correct legal knowledge claims that make the social existence of *law* – as opposed to mere *might* – possible.

This critical claim to objectivity is distinct from the objectivity of legal knowledge in a sociological sense. The latter is manifest in the social fact that people de facto claim to know what the law is. The critical claim is part of the social reality, without being coextensive with it. Much existing legal knowledge – and practice that is based upon it – may actually be utter nonsense.

> *Thinker*: The thinking of the subject is a part of the objective world, even if this thinking makes no sense at all.

---

[5] On the idea that knowledge of the world is part of the world, see, generally, M Gabriel, *Transcendental Ontology: Essays on German Idealism* (New York, Continuum, 2011) xii.

§ 7

The law, therefore, in order to be possible, must be based on sound legal knowledge; that is, on methods or procedures of knowing the law objectively in a critical sense.

> *Initiate*: Something is objectively known if the knowledge is true. Subjective knowledge is the state of mere believing regardless of whether the belief is true or false.

Any critical analysis of legal thinking attempts to determine how we can truly know what the law is. This concerns the format in which those professing knowledge of the law – scholars, practitioners – cast the law. Their knowledge, their 'scholarship', is tailored to the validation of legal claims that one person has against another.

Legal theory explores the possibility of legal knowledge that informs the adjudication of disputes. Such legal knowledge facilitates the application of legal standards to descriptions of sets of facts.

§ 8

> *Child*: This is a contract.
>
> *Judge*: How do you know?
>
> *Child*: I've seen it.
>
> *Judge (sighing)*: Oh, child!

§ 9

Legal knowledge must expect of itself to grasp the law correctly. This explains why the claim to the critical objectivity of legal knowledge is necessarily inherent in its social objectivity. Since the practice of legal knowledge mediates the existence of law, the critical dimension of this knowledge is inherent in the social existence of law. Without this dimension, there would be no law, but only a mass of unrelated and haphazard impositions on human conduct.

§ 10

From this *seems* to follow that legal systems, as long as they exist de facto, can owe their existence only to the correctness of legal knowledge, for there is nothing else that could bring about this existence. The very existence of law seems to demonstrate that the knowledge on which it is based must have been objective in the critical sense. So why bother about the critical dimension so long as the law is imagined into existence *somehow*?

> *Pupil*: I had the same question, but I did not dare ask.

> *Initiate*: Good grief!

Without objective knowledge in the critical sense there can be no law. The law exists. The existence of law is the living proof of the correctness of the knowledge mediating its existence. But why then worry about it as long as there is law?

> *Pupil*: Yes, let's scrap that critical dimension, it appears far too pungent anyway.

And yet, caution is required at this point. Before making premature concessions to objectively practised knowledge one needs to contemplate the possibility of encounters with law that is somehow incorrect. Such law either is merely apparent law – false law – or real law that misunderstands its own basis. It is law wearing ideological blinders.

§ 11

Conceivably, what purports to be law can in fact merely be power or money in disguise, such as in the case of the ascendancy of one class over another (see § 13). If its prerogatives are not supported by any sound arguments pointing to underlying legal right, but turn out to be mere expressions of political clout or an offshoot of wealth, then existing ('objective') legal knowledge provides only a camouflage for the operations of either power or money. There is, then, no legal system, but a timocracy or plutocracy in disguise. Law turns out to be either a variety of pursuing economic interests or of measures taken by the powerful.

Critics of the law have made such claims on several occasions:

> Your very ideas are but the outgrowth of the conditions of your bourgeois production and bourgeois property, just as your jurisprudence is but the will of your class made into a law for all, a will whose essential character and direction are determined by the economical [*sic*] conditions of existence of your class.[6]

---

[6] K Marx and F Engels, *Manifesto of the Communist Party* (London, William Reeves, 1988) 19.

The translation, obviously authorised by Engels, is so poor that I am taking my own stab at translating from the German original:

> Your very ideas are but the products of your bourgeois conditions of production and ownership, just as your law is merely the will of your class made into a law for all, a will whose substance is given in the material conditions of existence of your class.[7]

These critics have understood correctly that the validation of a claim to truth is not the same as the existence of a claim thereto. Existing claims must also be correct. Determining whether something is law is a matter of insight and not of buying – or having at one's service – expertise eager to whitewash machinations.

Under these circumstances, what is alleged to be law can turn out not to be law at all, at least upon closer inspection.

These circumstances have to be distinguished, however, from another form in which legal knowledge can go astray. It happens when it is mistaken about itself.

## § 12

Existing legal knowledge develops representations of itself and its own possibility. But it can simply be mistaken about that. Objective legal knowledge in the sociological sense may lack objectivity in the critical sense, even though it invariably has to lay claim to it (on the difference, see § 7). Nonetheless, it may still give rise to law on grounds that are different from what the knowers believe them to be. A critical analysis is then faced with the task of reconstructing the true basis of the knowledge that feeds into the creation of real law (see also § 60).

> *Judge (sighing, speaking into a voice recorder)*: From the system of values underlying the constitution it follows that a contract violating the order of creation is repugnant to law and justice.
>
> *Attorney (to an associate)*: Of course, this is all hokum. But the rules of procedure empower judges of a high court to invest all kinds of humbug with the force of law. What she says needs to be respected, even if she doesn't realise that this is the case only because she has said so and not because of her reasons for saying so.

---

[7] The basis of the translation is K Marx and F Engels, *Werke*, vol 4 (Berlin, Dietz Verlag, 1977) 477.

A judicial decision may believe itself to be intuiting the idea of justice. But what if there is no such thing as an immediate comprehension of right and wrong? It may then be concluded that the authority of the decision is in fact derivative of the legal power of an institution to draw legally binding conclusions from a supposed 'vision' of ideas.

> *Pupil*: How is it then possible for the judiciary to produce socially objective legal knowledge while, from a critical perspective, the judges are in error about what they do in fact?

It must be possible to produce law on the basis of false understandings of it, for there could be no legal system if all applied legal knowledge had to be correct. Not only is such correctness invariably contested, its conditions are subject to divergent elaborations that are bound to conflict because they are loaded with philosophy.

The condition for the existence of law is not, then, that the socially objective knowledge must *always* also be objective in a critical sense (see § 10), but rather that, as stated above (see § 9), the *concern* with critical objectivity must be part of what is objective knowledge in a sociological sense. Indeed, within legal systems it remains indeterminate what the correct knowledge claims are. But law-applying officials have to be concerned with applying real law, for otherwise they could be told that what they do is merely allowing the manoeuvres of money and power to have their way. Since objectively valid knowledge is what *definitely* mediates the existence of law, legal knowledge must take an interest in its objectivity in a critical sense. Otherwise, it could not claim to be about law (see § 7 and § 9).

Since there would be no law without legal knowledge (see § 1) and legal knowledge must aim at the truth, exploring the conditions of truth is part the existence of law (see § 14). No law without legal theory.

## § 13

None of the above affects the fact that *all* socially objective legal knowledge – regardless of whether or not it generates merely apparent law (see § 11) or law that misunderstands its foundation (see § 12) – is aided and abetted by the operations of money or power. It must be economically reasonable to go to court. One had better abstain from wasting one's energies on causes that look hopeless from the outset because the existing jurisprudence appears to be dead set against them.

It is not by coincidence, then, that the value of legal knowledge is reflected in other media than truth.

Above all, it reflects on its value in the medium of *money*. From this perspective, legal knowledge is made available as a service the provision of which requires a marketable skill. What counts is not its ability to know the law objectively, but its ability to create demand for legal expertise.

> *Pupil*: Should I attend a course on legal logic?
>
> *Judge*: Waste of time; it is smarter to take a class on commercial arbitration. It looks better on your transcript.

Legal knowledge reflects on its value also from the perspective of power in that it understands itself as a means of achieving goals. It thus comes to perceive itself as a tool that can be used to control others.

> *Attorney (to pupil)*: We're gonna figure out the brain of that weirdo judge and then we're gonna win this case.

Much intellectual space in law is subject to the influence of social *power*. Take, for example, methods of statutory construction used by the highest courts. For anyone affected by their jurisprudence, there is no way around using them in practice, no matter how foolish they may seem. Their relevance forces everyone who wants to be successful in a court to abide slavishly by accepted routines. Even if a method is unfounded, socially it remains firmly in the saddle as long as the courts support it. The result is either false law, ie a mere pretence on the part of political power (see § 11), or real law that has its true basis in the decision-making power of a supreme court (see § 12).

## § 14

Questions of legal theory can be traced back to the core question of the conditions under which legal statements can be true.[8] Answering this question presupposes answering a number of others.

First, legal theory asks in the usual drawn-out way, 'What is law'? Obviously, legal knowledge has to avail of an *object*. It is in this context, that one also encounters the problem of *legal validity*.

---

[8] The core question of whether legal statements are true is at the centre of Dennis Patterson's work *Law and Truth* (New York, Oxford University Press, 1996).

Second, legal theory examines how capable or potent legal knowledge is by asking how far its claim to *objectivity* can extend. Does it merely pertain to positive law or also to what is amenable to insight on the basis of practical reason alone – natural law, that is?[9] In the same context, the 'depth' of legal knowledge is at stake. Is it able to offer a *right answer* to every legal question or is there reason for greater modesty? Furthermore, the *systematicity* of legal knowledge is a recurring theme.

Third, the exploration of how capable or potent legal knowledge is raises questions concerning its *modal status*. Is legal knowledge based on conceptually necessary principles or is it historically contingent? The less trust one has in its ability to reveal the truth, the more legal theories tend towards some kind of conventionalism.

## § 15

Legal theory has a history. One has to be familiar with this history in order to understand the challenges that the discipline has prepared for itself.

It is no coincidence that the history of legal theory begins at the moment when the critical objectivity of legal knowledge first became deeply doubtful. This moment is marked by the decline of the last specimen of *scientia iuris*, namely the legal formalism of the late nineteenth and early twentieth centuries. The longer and broader tradition of legal science, however, dates all the way back to the Middle Ages.

In retrospect, this legal formalism, also known as 'conceptual jurisprudence' or 'conceptualism', appears like a golden age of legal scholarship. The systematic penetration of legal materials was supposed to reassure scholars of their ability to say what the law is in individual cases. Systematisation would take care of seeming gaps. It should be possible to find the right answer to every legal question by exploring all the corners of the system in a 'formal' manner, ie without evaluating anything from a moral point of view. From the European tradition of *scientia iuris*, legal formalism adopted the idea that legal knowledge and its subject matter are 'autonomous'. One consequence of this autonomy was the belief that there is a method of legal knowledge – legal scholarship – that is intrinsic to the law itself.

---

[9] For a famous rejuvenation of natural law theory in the late twentieth century, see J Finnis, *Natural Law and Natural Rights* (Oxford, Clarendon Press, 1980).

The second chapter of this book is devoted to legal formalism. At the turn of the nineteenth and twentieth centuries, this conception of legal knowledge was subject to sharp criticism, which is laid out in the third chapter. The unsettling of formalism explains why a refined version of legal positivism came to play the key role in the theory of legal knowledge in the course of the twentieth century. That is what the fourth chapter is about.

The relevant connections can be made intelligible from a stylised historical telling that satisfies the demand of a rational reconstruction better than the actual history. The point of view is, admittedly, somewhat artificial.

## § 16

This better story comprises three phases.

The first phase begins with the criticism of legal formalism during the first three decades of the twentieth century. This criticism is voiced from the midst of the German free law movement and American legal realism. The latter is particularly sobering. All formalistic legal knowledge is dismissed as 'transcendental nonsense'. It is exposed as amounting to nothing, or rather, as an appearance without reality. It needs to be replaced with the explanation of judicial behaviour. The judges themselves are supposed to decide cases on the basis of moral or economic considerations. Legal questions can only be rationally dealt with from the perspective of discourses that are not 'legal'. Legal knowledge is dismissed as being deeply chimerical.

This shake-up of established jurisprudence caused by legal realism profoundly shapes the intellectual climate of legal scholarship in the USA to this day. In order to be regarded as intellectually respectable, any study of law that is not merely 'doctrinal' has to explore legal phenomena from the perspective of the social sciences, such as economics and sociology, or have recourse to practical philosophy.

## § 17

From an (admittedly, historically somewhat constructed) perspective on the challenge provided by the realist critique, Hans Kelsen's version of legal positivism – which is under gestation at about the same time that realism is wreaking havoc – can be understood as the attempt to save what can be saved from legal scholarship in the face of what has been rightly identified as its severe shortcomings. According to Kelsen, the ideas that can be rescued include the normativity of law (in contrast to the reduction of legal norms to the 'patterns of judicial behaviour') and its systematic quality (in contrast to the image of a patchwork of legislative decisions or individual acts).

Kelsen, however, also drops important elements from the formalist repertoire. For that reason, his theory bears a family resemblance to the realists. Kelsen also tries to uncover the political ideology behind the formalist mumbo jumbo. This uncovering of the political ideology concerns, for example, the allegedly 'apolitical' and domination-free nature of private legal relations. Kelsen and the American legal realist Robert Hale can join hands in this respect.[10] Also, what formalism – endorsing the dogma of the completeness of the legal system – claimed to amount to a 'scientific' discovery of law is reconstructed by Kelsen as politically informed law creation that has to stay within a margin of discretion.

Nevertheless, Kelsen aspires to build a 'pure' theory of law. He aims to distinguish legal thinking from both empirical social research and moral reasoning. The normativist tenor of his theory creates a clear distance from legal realism. This critical attitude towards legal realism is still reflected in the writings of the important British legal positivist H.L.A. Hart, whose most influential works appeared in the 1950s and 1960s. However, the partial compatibility with the realist critique is not abundantly clear in his case. A possible explanation is that Hart did not have to struggle with the legacy of continental European legal formalism in the United Kingdom.

## § 18

The second phase initially sees legal positivism at its scintillating climax. Its success in the Anglo-American tradition is manifest in the legacy of Hart's theory, a legacy that continues to this day. The triumph of legal positivism is not least owing to the fact that Hart is taken to have succeeded in translating Kelsen's ideas into the idiom of ordinary language philosophy.

The attendant assimilation with common sense, however, comes at a cost. Legal positivism loses its critical bite and seems to keep legal realism at arm's length (see § 16). It loses its focus on the problem of legal

---

[10] See RL Hale, 'Bargaining, Duress, and Economic Liberty' (1943) 43 *Columbia Law Review* 603–28. On Hale, see BH Fried, *The Progressive Assault on Laissez Faire: Robert Hale and the First Law and Economics Movement* (Cambridge, MA, Harvard University Press, 1998); N Duxbury, 'Robert Hale and the Economy of Legal Force' (1990) 53 *Modern Law Review* 421–44.

knowledge and becomes a scholastic discipline mostly dealing with self-made problems.

The second phase ends with the internal collapse of the legal positivist position. This is what the fifth chapter is about. Since modern positivism exists in both continental and Anglo-American formats, it is, unsurprisingly, plagued by two requisite versions of immanent critique. While in continental Europe the critique leads straight into social systems theory, in the Anglo-American world it results in something resembling a renaissance of natural law theory.

But the collapse of continental legal positivism began early, starting in the 1920s. It is first manifest in the works of the *enfant terrible* of Kelsen's Viennese School, Fritz Sander. His analyses anticipate much of what sociological systems theorists such as Niklas Luhmann and Gunther Teubner would later reintroduce into the discussion.

The Anglo-American dismantling of legal positivism is carried out most prominently in the early work of Ronald Dworkin. It had been anticipated decades earlier, namely in Carl Schmitt's institutionalist legal theory of law. Schmitt himself was taking his cue from the work of the French public law scholar Maurice Hauriou. The institutionalists and Dworkin emphasise that the law is 'objective spirit', by which we mean an institutionally shared way of justifying behaviour that reflects on and examines its own authority while it is being practised. The sixth chapter explores this way of thinking.

§ 19

The third phase, in which legal theory still finds itself today, can thus rightly be described as 'post-positivist'. It addresses the question of what conclusion can be drawn from the heroic failure of the legal positivist project.

Ironically enough, the path taken by Dworkin leads back to central positions of formalism. Dworkin postulates that there is a substantively right answer to every legal question. In this respect, he conjures up the golden age of legal scholarship, even if with greater intellectual circumspection. Although the legal system is again understood as comprehensive and complete, Dworkin no longer sustains the separation of law and morality.

Once the spectre of formalism is raised, the realist criticism is not long in coming. The seventh chapter is dedicated to its recrudescence, which used the banner of 'Critical Legal Studies'. Apart from 'Law and Economics', the 'Crits' were the most important legal-theoretical trend of the late twentieth century. Their representatives took issue with the belief in a morally informed right answer. They arrived at a view of a moral consciousness that is rife with antinomies and irreconcilably divided into conflicting altruistic and individualistic moral intuitions. In the end, all aspiration to correctness is replaced with rhetorical masquerade. Even if 'deconstruction' is often invoked in this context, what really prevails is romantic irony, especially since all legal knowledge becomes dissolved into the free play of artful arguments and counterarguments that are all bound to remain inclusive. The result is fundamental legal indeterminacy.

§ 20

The legal theory of the present has not at all resolved the post-positivist situation of collapse.

The irony with which Critical Legal Studies rejects the serious demeanour of legal knowledge indicates that its approach has retained a central element of legal positivism, namely the detachment of legal knowledge from law as an object of study. This detachment is the key to developing a post-positivist theory of legal knowledge. Its relevance, however, needs to be grasped more radically than legal positivism has ever been able to do. What needs to be understood, still, is that the detachment from the object is, as it were, inherent in this object itself.

The task of reconstruction can be accomplished by conceiving of the law as a certain relation between and among people. The eighth chapter concludes the book with reflections on this topic.

The remaining sections of the current chapter attempt to lay the foundation of this shift to the legal relation and thereby anticipate the conclusion of the book. They are premised on the idea that knowing the law is indeed a way of knowing what one ought to do. The law provides us with practical knowledge. This knowledge originates, however, from a mode of relating to one another that represents the reasons of other people as sources of law.

§ 21

A human relationship lends expression to the legal relation once people abstain from making direct moral demands on one another and mutually confine themselves to allowing each other's claims to go forward, albeit within limits.[11] In other words, they thus ascribe rights to each other. The 'As a reasonable person you really should …' is thereby transmuted into 'You shall … because I want it'. Or 'People ought to live in a godly manner' becomes 'Respect the lifestyle that others consider to be godly'.

The form of the legal relation is determined by yielding to reasons that others find convincing. What may appear imperative to you does not force me to agree with you. Rather, it *seems* to me that what convinces you is just your choice. What you feel you must do is rendered for me in the medium of the legal relation as your choice. It appears as a choice to me because for me there is nothing persuasive in what may sway you.

That is why the room that we concede to others when we yield to what seems to be convincing to them expands *intersubjectively* from the inside into the room of haphazard choices. It is rendered socially as room for manoeuvring in which freedom can unfold.

*The other*: That's what you have decided, and that's all right.

## § 22

The emergence of the legal relation is accompanied by a remarkable transformation of practical reason. It is in my choices that you encounter the *other* reason of someone who is your equal.

I really want to have a car with 560 horsepower. You consider such a desire to be outright absurd. But you respect that rational beings can have desires that you believe to be somewhat crazy. You do not exclude the persons concerned – me, for that matter – from the set of reasonable people.

Your reasons for respecting my bad practical reasons are good practical reasons. If such reasons make us show each other respect, we can get along. I still pass in your eyes as a rational self and in this respect as capable of responding to reasons.

---

[11] First expositions of the idea that legal theory is the theory of legal knowledge can be found in G Pavlakos, *Our Knowledge of the Law: Objectivity and Practice in Legal Theory* (Oxford, Hart Publishing, 2007) and my book *Rechtliches Wissen* (Frankfurt aM, Suhrkamp, 2006). The scaffolding of the whole approach is now laid out in my *Wissen des Rechts* (Tübingen, Mohr, 2018).

§ 23

There is, however, a hermeneutic gulf separating you and me. What makes sense to me appears strange to you. I am red, you are blue. I am not like you.

> *Reader:* Could you explain to me what you mean by 'hermeneutic'?

> *Author (clearing his throat):* Sure, uhm, 'hermeneutic' is any effort to understand signs, utterances, ways of thinking or behaviours that one does not understand at first glance.

But you also understand that what I think and how I think, at least so long as you acknowledge me as an equal, could be an expression of reason. You would just have to be somebody else in order to regard this reason as your own. In my thinking you encounter your own practical reason embodied differently. Moral values have a different weight. Relevancies diverge. This has an effect on what is considered justified in certain cases.

Taking up an expression first coined by Michael Theunissen to designate the encounter with alterity in an intersubjective context, this phenomenon can be called 'altered reason'.[12] The encounter with such reason indicates the existence of a hermeneutic gulf.

The reciprocity of morality requires that you consider yourself a self with altered reason among others. Viewed from the web of relations to others, you become another of yourself.

§ 24

The hermeneutic gulf is not a purely interpersonal affair. It is also intrapersonal. I am stuck in routines and do not understand why. I buy books despite knowing that I will never be able to read them. My behaviour seems pointless. I prefer listening to operas to playing squash. There's no good reason for that, except that 'I have become who I am'. But that does not really explain my conduct. It signifies the dearth of an explanation.

I am carrying a hermeneutic gulf within me. I don't understand myself. But why should I care? Sometimes I get along better with myself if I do

---

[12] The term 'altered' is a clumsy reference to *verandert* (and *Veranderung*), which can be found in M Theunissen, *Der Andere: Studien zur Sozialontologie der Gegenwart*, 2nd edn (Berlin, de Gruyter, 1977). In fact, the term was created from the German verb *verändern*, which means to change, by taking the *Umlaut* out. This is how *anders* (being different or other) is captured in the meaning of the word. In my mind, the English 'alter' conjures up the 'alter ego', which explains why I thought I could use it.

not examine the grounds of my conduct. My relation to myself then simply *anticipates* the legal relation.

## § 25

> *She*: Which photo should we take for the invitation? The one with or the one without the sky?
>
> *He*: I don't care.
>
> *She*: But you have to make a choice.
>
> *He*: Then we'll take the one without the sky.
>
> *She*: But, isn't that too gloomy?
>
> *He*: Then we'll take the one with the sky.

Sometimes we are occupied by a deep hermeneutic void.

## § 26

You believe my desire to own a car with 560 horsepower is a sign of madness. In your view, my own frivolity is supported by legislation that fails to prevent it. Thus, there is not only a fissure of understanding between you and me, but also a hermeneutic gulf separating you from the legislature.

What is authoritative, even though it is not necessary, is merely posited. Legal norms are products of history. They are ontologically in the same category as traditions or mentalities. We respect them because we have to stick to something in order to get along.

## § 27

With that we are getting to the most difficult point.

> *Reader*: Now this is getting scary.

The law allows for the social constitution of altered reason (see § 23) and is one of its products. That is why what we know to be law comes into this world in the form of sources.

To understand this, one must bear in mind that respect for decisions – an exercise of freedom of choice – bridges the hermeneutic gulf without closing it. It is possible to connect without establishing a connection to the reasons for action.

§ 28

*Politician*: We do not want to see any headscarves in our schools.

*Thinker*: This is an implication of the principle of secularity.

*Teacher*: Politics wants no one to wear a headscarf. *(She takes a deep breath)*. Great. But if this is really about suppressing any religious symbolism, any other symbol lending expression to faith will have to be ousted from schools, too. Super. And we have to face the music.

The hermeneutic gulf is bridged by an effort to come to terms with what one does not understand. This effort *accepts* the altered reason and treats it *as if* it were a proper one. It preserves the gulf by regarding as a decision what the persons concerned may view as their insight.

*Initiate*: I hear you have decided to attend the next performance of Wagner's *Rheingold*.

*Pupil*: I must, I am a card-carrying Wagnerian.

*Thinker*: But does not this example demonstrate that there is no gulf? Why can't a counterfactual bridge the gap? Why not say that if I were a Wagnerian, I would have reason to go? I thereby said that I understand all Wagnerians to have a reason. It is just a reason relative to persons.

*Poet*: My guess is that the hermeneutic gulf is nested in the condition 'If I were …'. Do I, or does anyone, have reason to be what I subjunctively can be? – Oh, lovely, what a sentence!

§ 29

If we really want something, we transform ourselves into a means of realising a purpose.[13] Because I want air conditioning, I contact an air conditioning company. In the course of the conversation with their representative it becomes clear to me that my wish can be realised. A few days later, I sign a contract. Through the contractual commitment, I have made myself – or rather, my conduct – into a means of realising the purpose.

---

[13] The account of volition offered here is deeply indebted to CM Korsgaard, *Self-Constitution: Action, Identity, and Integrity* (Oxford, Oxford University Press, 2009).

My will is the result of a period of reflection, at the end of which I attain what I take to be clarity. From this perspective, my pondering and contemplating have seamlessly grown into what I want to do.

§ 30

But this is just the way it seems to me because I have not really detached myself from this particular desire and also abstained from consulting the more awkward precincts of my conscience. Had I considered my wish against the background of others and weighed up what is really important to me, my desire to have air conditioning would likely have appeared to be a decision, especially if this wish cannot reasonably be compared with any competitor in the quiver of my desires. Hence, upon reflection it could turn out that I have actually *decided* to get air conditioning instead of studying theology.

> *Reader*: Wow!

> *Author*: This is only a hypothetical example. In reality, the choice was exceedingly more agonising, namely between air conditioning and a car featuring 560 horsepower.

A decision marks the end of a period of ratiocination. However, it somehow also repeals it or retroactively suspends its relevance. It emancipates the reasoner from being pulled back and forth by conflicting reasons. By formulating a summons, the decision directs us to move forward. Upon looking back, we often discover a hermeneutic gulf and ask ourselves:

> *We*: But why on earth …?

Nonetheless, a decision is a move that allows one to know what to do. We make up our mind. There is knowing that is mediated by insight. But there is also knowing that stems from transcending the vain hope of arriving at insight.

Knowing something to be right for good reasons and knowing something because one has made up one's mind can entirely depend on the perspective. What matters, however, in our context, is that the legal relation is thus constituted that regardless of whether people may find something convincing or inevitable, what they set their mind to is rendered for others as a choice. They may believe they know what is right, but their knowledge is intersubjectively validated only if it is cast as stemming from a source of legal authority. What may be known by one can have authority for the other if it is viewed as choice.

## § 31

Up to this point, we have used the concept 'legal knowledge' for statements that are tailored to fit situations in which people raise, defend or adjudicate legal claims. Now the concept can be expanded to include sources of law. Broadly understood, then, legal knowledge means knowing our obligations and rights authoritatively in the form of choices or decisions.

In the case of customary law, the knowledge claim inherent in the legal source emerges with great clarity.[14] The most plausible way of perceiving custom as a source of law consists of seeing it based on shared intuitions. A group reassures itself of the fact that a conviction is shared among its members by referring to its manifestations over time. The practice is the proof. The conviction is what matters. The knowledge of law inherent in the shared conviction is entirely intuitive. From a second-personal perspective it is on a plane with a decision because it appears to come out of nowhere.

> *Custom*: We don't allow this to happen here. We have never allowed this.

Recognising intuitions or decisions bridges the uncanny hermeneutic gulf that arises within customary law itself. Whence the shared conviction? The easy answer, which does not answer anything, is that it originates from the 'spirit of the people'.

> *Pupil*: Gee, I did not know that.

But even if those involved in customary practice harboured elaborate philosophical views about what grounds it rests upon, these views would not matter. By speaking of customary law, we acknowledge as their choice – or rather, their intuition – what folks understand to be their shared knowledge of the law even though there is no other warrant for it than regular practice.

To me my decision to have air conditioning installed emerges quite naturally from my desires and available resources. It is 'logical', as long as

---

[14] The theory of legal sources developed in this introduction is inspired by FC von Savigny, *On the Vocation of Our Time for Legislation and Jurisprudence* (trans AH Abraham, London, Littlewood, 1831) and GF Puchta, *Das Gewohnheitsrecht*, vol 1 (Erlangen, Palmsche Verlagsbuchhandlung, 1828); vol 2 (Erlangen, Palmsche Verlagsbuchhandlung, 1837).

I don't step outside the tunnel vision of this particular desire. When I examine it against the background of my life as a whole and when I compare it with having to defer my exploration of theological trials and tribulations, it appears to have emancipated me from the unending to and fro of considering potentially incommensurate benefits and costs.

§ 32

> *Child*: I know I must have an ice cream because I have such a strong longing for it.
>
> *Mother*: Why are you expressing yourself in such a complicated way! Just say that you would like to have some.

§ 33

Legal scholarship is a source of law. Admittedly, this idea is not particularly well received in – and outside of – legal circles. It is either detested as an elitist charade or rejected as utter nonsense. Resistance to truth does not, however, in and of itself detract from it.

Ostensibly, provided that it is a source, legal scholarship is of a second-order variety, for it works with material from other sources. Hence, legal knowledge, narrowly understood (see § 31), is knowledge of other knowledge. Knowing what one knows implies, however, being able to assess its validity and relevance.

There is, hence, a noteworthy difference between custom and legislation (see § 34), on the one hand, and scholarship, on the other. Legal knowledge comes to its completion once we can say who has a claim against whom or who is obligated to do or to forbear from what. Assuming that there was no scholarship *qua* second-order source, the first-order sources would have to speak for themselves:

> *Custom*: We don't allow this to happen here! We have never allowed this!
>
> *Legislation*: But we have already said that we don't permit this!

The sources articulate their practical knowledge with the authority intrinsic to the source and do not talk *about* what thereby emerges from them. The question of whether or not it is appropriate to apply a particular norm does not even arise because there is no way of distinguishing between the application and the creation of law. They are one and the same and therefore neither.

> *Custom*: We don't allow this to happen here!

Is this the application of custom as a norm or is the one final assertion necessary to make it into what it is? Or is perhaps the assertion necessary to sustain custom as a binding standard?

> *Legislation*: But we have already said that we don't permit this!

Even if the legislation is mistaken about its doings, it has now said what it wants.

The exploration of the conditions under which it is appropriate to apply a norm begins when legal scholarship enters the scene. It puts other practical knowledge that is legally known in its proper place. It recasts the law in a manner that makes it applicable to individual cases by determining circumstances in which it is appropriate to apply one rather than another provision in certain situations. This involves calibrating their substantive scope of application with an eye to their attachment to a set of potentially competing or conflicting norms. The relevant findings made by legal scholarship amount to universalisation across the relevant set.

> *Initiate*: In each case of *x*, rule *y* ought to be applied.

In order to accomplish this task, legal scholarship develops an array of highly sophisticated conceptual distinctions. The point of these distinctions is to identify normatively significant differences that are relevant to the classification of factual situations.

> *Initiate*: The cases of liability for a positive breach of contract differ
> from cases of an implied warranty as follows …

Legal scholarship is a wellspring of legal knowledge. But it is also a genuine source of law. This is the case insofar as this knowledge is a product of interpretive and conceptual choices that are not derivative of the substance of legal norms. Such choices are inevitable since in the process of legal application, the scope of application of several legal provisions has to be determined in relation to one another, or the meaning of certain legal terms (such as 'negligent') has to be drawn out at a level of greater detail. Such an elaboration of the substance of law also transforms it. The norms become recast in a different format. Their meaning becomes converted into elements of analytical grids that are supposed to guide the analysis of individual cases. Such constructions are indispensable in order to bring the law as closely as possible to the facts.

In this context, legal scholarship is, as the Germans say, 'dogmatic'. Nobody is in the position to reinvent the wheel. Everyone works with ideas that have proven to be useful in the past. The law that is constructed by drawing on conventional wisdom (*dogmata*) grows historically and is not based on compelling insight. Its growth involves decisions.

## § 34

What is known by legislation? Doesn't the view of sources as forms of legal knowledge come to an end here?

Legislation claims to know how we ought to move forward. Since that claim is rejected by anyone opposed to its laws, the practical knowledge of legislation obviously must be regarded as a decision. Of course, in various instances legislation is merely a systematic summary of case law. In such a case it obviously has its roots in legal scholarship.

Any source of law is knowledge that originates from 'making up one's mind' (see § 30). The relevance of a decisional element indicates that knowledge has to bridge a hermeneutic gulf. We know what the legislature has said by *giving* it a certain reading. We know what we want because we have *taken a vote*. We know what we believe to be right because we have always *seen* it this way (and this seeing is manifest in past and present practice).

## § 35

With an eye to legal scholarship's ambition to cast the law in a manner that renders it most easily applicable to individual cases, legal sources can be arranged in a sequence. In passing through this sequence, the law becomes ever more clearly and better known.

Customary law is burdened with a great deal of obscurity. How much practice is needed and who has to engage in it? Who must be convinced? How can practice be put into a rule? Legislation absorbs this uncertainty by basing the creation of norms on clear decision-making rules that lead to the adoption of written laws. But those laws do not apply themselves to facts. The final stage of clarification of legal knowledge is achieved at the level of legal scholarship. What it does (not least by relying on common wisdom) is ultimately grounded in intellectual habits – customs, in a sense.

One does not have to put customary law at the beginning of this sequence. One could equally start with the mutually shared awareness that the constitution is valid law. Such awareness, however, would have to be regarded as knowledge that involves a decision.

§ 36

In legal scholarship we encounter the subjectivity of law in its most fully fledged form, for it embodies the comparatively highest degree of rationality. Custom intuits the law, legislation chooses to adopt it in the pursuit of political objectives, legal scholarship arrives, where possible, at elaborate arguments concerning the proper scope of the application of laws. But since all law is conveyed through legal knowledge (see § 1), it becomes objectified – a historical reality – on the basis of being known by someone.

Legal scholarship is something historical. In the final event, it also is based on choices to let us know something in a certain way.

Against this background, the question must arise whether it is possible for legal scholarship to sustain its claim to objectivity in a critical sense. Is there any guidance left in the face of pervasive historical contingency?

The legal knowledge produced in legal scholarship has to be consistent with the legal relation. This is a relation among 'abstract' persons. It is presupposed that they are facing each other without revealing their histories or beliefs. They are unknown to one another. In a way, they are the same, just equal agents with rights and obligations. Equality is a core principle of the legal relation.

Not by accident, equality underpins the calibration of the scope of application of norms. Each case should be treated equally from the perspective of a system of norms. The systematisation represents the critical touchstone of legal knowledge that is objective in a critical sense. System building is indispensable for legal scholarship. Without it, it would not be possible to select from an array of applicable norms the one that fits a particular type of case. Without system building, all that one would be left with would amount to mere intuitionism.

*Judge*: I like that rule. I'll apply it to the case at hand.

## § 37

This is not to say, however, that systematic legal scholarship has to clothe the law in a most appealing moral garb. This would be inconsistent with legality as the default mode of compliance within a legal relation.

Legality, as understood by Kant, means the 'external' observance of norms.[15] Conduct does not presuppose, and cannot be required to involve, identification with their content. This is a consequence of the hermeneutic gulf.

The detached attitude of legality is legitimately manifest in knowledge that claims to know what the law is. Constructing the law with an eye to the fundamental idea of equal treatment does not at all involve identification with the substance of norms. Rather, the key to understanding the critical dimension of legal knowledge is serene irony.[16]

## § 38

The paradigm of this type of irony is the interpretation of works of literature or philosophy. It is an effort to understand the imagination or the thinking of another person. For example, interpreters engage in an effort to grasp the reasoning of a master thinker. Often, this concerns eminent philosophers such as Kant or Wittgenstein. The interpreter of the work usually tends to demonstrate what challenges the master faced and how he or she went about mastering them. In this process of interpretation, a lot of energy is invested in giving the work an impressive appearance.

Identification with the thoughts of the master, however, is not necessarily on the cards. Ultimately, the interpreter may reserve the right to dissociate himself from the thinker's thoughts. Keeping the claims of the master at arm's length is always an option. It is conceivable for the interpreter to arrive at the conclusion that the work ultimately falls short. The

---

[15] See I Kant, *The Metaphysics of Morals* (trans M Gregor, Cambridge, Cambridge University Press, 2017) A 15. I only had the German version available: I Kant, *Die Metaphysik der Sitten*, Werkausgabe vol 8 (ed W Weischedel, Frankfurt aM, Insel, 1968) 324 (A 15).

[16] For a first discussion of this matter, see my *The Legal Relation: Legal Theory After Legal Positivism* (Cambridge, Cambridge University Press, 2017) 128, 130–31.

work of dangerous thinkers is not infrequently approached with the attitude of 'incredibly impressive, but it cannot be true'.

§ 39

If legal knowledge understood itself correctly, it would openly admit to serene irony as its mood. The lack of seriousness that goes along with it is not a shortcoming. In fact, it is serious. For it reminds us of the hermeneutic gulf that separates us from the law and from one another in the medium of the legal relation.

Serene irony is legality of behaviour in the context of legal interpretation. It is indicative of practical reason reaching out beyond itself. The attendant aesthetic illusion is not a deficiency, but lends expression to a playful completion of the normative as a result of which it becomes stripped of its oppressive tinge.

# Mild and Wild Formalism

## § 40

What do we mean by 'formalism' in the context of law?[1]

In a historically specific sense, this concept is linked to an idea that was held in high regard at the end of the nineteenth century.[2] Puzzlingly, this idea concerns the substance of the law. Formal law is law that provides the vessels that freely choosing legal subjects are able to fill with content as they themselves see fit. They can do so, of course, only within limits and with responsibility and liability attached. From the perspective of nineteenth-century legal formalism, the law consists essentially of rules governing voluntary transactions and norms concerning liability. By using these forms, legal entities can, within certain limits, regulate what they want; and based on liability rules they can claim compensation for damages suffered.

The paradigm of a voluntary binding transaction is the contract. It can be used for a variety of purposes. From a formalistic point of view, legal knowledge must abstain from morally evaluating these purposes. Whether a landlord exercises his rights against his tenant in a morally equitable manner is legally irrelevant so long as he only makes use of his rights on the basis of, and in accordance with, a valid contractual agreement.

The law allows the pursuit of interests and grants the power to make choices (see § 21). Issues of application are to be clarified by recourse to the relevant legal conditions. That is why one encounters in formalism a sharp demarcation between legal reasoning proper on the one hand and the morally open-minded weighing of interests or values on the other.[3]

---

[1] A good beginning for familiarising oneself with the formalist emphasis on rules and constraints by language is F Schauer, 'Formalism' (1988) 97 *Yale Law Journal* 509–48.

[2] On the German version of conceptual jurisprudence (*Begriffsjurisprudenz*) see the anthology by W Krawietz (ed), *Theorie und Technik der Begriffsjurisprudenz* (Darmstadt, Wissenschaftliche Buchgesellschaft, 1976). For prominent criticism of this way of thinking see E Ehrlich, *Die juristische Logik*, 2nd edn (Tübingen, Mohr, 1925). Good introductions to the topic are offered by U Falk, *Ein Gelehrter wie Windscheid: Erkundungen auf dem Gebiet der sogenannten Begriffsjurisprudenz* (Frankfurt aM, Klostermann, 1989); HP Haverkamp, *Georg Friedrich Puchta und die 'Begriffsjurisprudenz'* (Frankfurt aM, Klostermann, 2004); T Henkel, *Begriffsjurisprudenz und Billigkeit: Zum Rechtsformalismus der Pandektistik nach G. F. Puchta* (Cologne, Böhlau, 2004); CE Mecke, *Begriff und System des Rechts bei Georg Friedrich Puchta* (Göttingen, V & R unipress, 2009).

[3] On 'formalism' in the history of American law, see TC Grey, 'Langdell's Orthodoxy' (1983) 45 *University of Pittsburgh Law Review* 1–53, reprinted in S Brewer (ed), *The Philosophy of Legal Reasoning: A Collection of*

Formalists believe that legal issues can be resolved in a 'value-free' manner. Private individuals or political bodies make the value choices. They thereby pour substance into the vessels of legal forms. Legal knowledge needs to pay keen attention to the law-creating effect of the use of these forms.

## § 41

Formalists usually translate the expectation which free agents have towards the law into an expectation concerning its linguistic form. The law ought to be calculable. Let it be as predictable as the 'amen' in a prayer.

The predictability of the application is to be effected, among other things, by a precise rendering of the law's content. This explains why formalists prefer legal rules, the application of which is conditioned by empirically ascertainable facts that do not require unreliable interpretation (eg an interpretation of the motives of a criminal defendant). They take unclear language as implicitly empowering those expounding the law.

> *Pupil*: Isn't the rule according to which a contract may not offend against 'morality' meaningless?

> *Initiate*: Not at all; it means, plainly and simply, that the courts are empowered to determine by their own lights whether a relevant violation has occurred.

The preference for clarity is reflected in a certain expectation that formalists often harbour towards language. Stanley Fish characterised it to the effect that, from their point of view, the law itself wishes to assume a 'formal existence'. The law strives to look 'independent' and 'natural'. Moral judgement and interpretive construction endanger this form of existence. They threaten to undo the supposed permanence and universality of the law. As Fish puts it:

> Formalism is the thesis that it is possible to put down marks so self-sufficiently perspicuous that they repel interpretation; it is the thesis that one can write sentences of such precision and simplicity that their meanings leap off the page in a way no one – no matter what his or her situation of point of view – can ignore; it is the thesis that one can devise procedures

*Essays by Philosophers and Legal Scholars* (London, Routledge, 1998) 115–67; N Duxbury, *Patterns of American Jurisprudence* (Oxford, Oxford University Press, 1995) 9–64. For an account that tries to take both sides of the North Atlantic equally into account, see K Tuori, *Ratio and Voluntas: The Tension Between Reason and Will in the Law* (Farnham, Ashgate, 2011) 75–144.

that are self-executing in the sense that their unfolding is independent of the differences between the agents who might set them in motion. In the presence (in the strong Derridean sense) of such a mark or sentence or procedure, the interpretive will is stopped short and is obliged to press its claims within the constraints provided by that which it cannot override. It must take the marks into account; it must respect the self-declaring reasons; it must follow the route laid down by the implacable procedures, and if it then wins it will have done duly, with justice, with reason.[4]

Fish does not support this view. In his work, he tries to demonstrate that the impression of clarity can only be created by means of denying a previous ambiguity. Thus, the impression of clear contractual language can only be brought about by an interpretation that implicitly and tacitly appeals to the moral convictions of the addressees. In his view, formalism can be effective only if scholars possess the requisite rhetorical skills to suppress the non-formal means by which the law takes on a formal existence (for example by referring to an 'obvious meaning of a word').

## § 42

The expectation concerning language aside, one associates formalism above all with a deductive style of reasoning that has been denigrated by its critics as 'conceptual jurisprudence'.

The basic idea of 'conceptual jurisprudence' is as simple as it is captivating. Specific legal phenomena, such as contracts, are based upon legal phenomena of a greater generality, such as 'legal transactions'. In cases of doubt, the application of specific phenomena has to have recourse to a relatively more general level. This is where one will find an answer.

> *Pupil*: Can a contract offer be accepted by providing the expected performance in return?
>
> *Initiate*: This question can only be answered by keeping in mind what the acceptance of an offer is, legally speaking.
>
> *Pupil*: Usually, an acceptance is made by declaring one's will.
>
> *Initiate*: Sure. But what is the performance of the service?
>
> *Pupil*: A manifestation of one's will?

---

[4] S Fish, 'The Law Wishes to Have a Formal Existence' in his *There's No Such Thing as Free Speech* (New York and Oxford, Oxford University Press, 1994) 141–79, 142–43.

*Initiate*: Thus, the question arises …

*Pupil*: … whether a contractual offer can be accepted by a mere manifestation of one's will, even though such conduct does not amount to a declaration.

*Initiate*: What do we need to know in order to answer this question?

*Pupil*: We must know what a contract is.

*Initiate*: And what is a contract?

*Pupil*: A contract is a legal transaction composed of two complementary legal transactions.

*Initiate*: Is a declaration of will a legal transaction?

*Pupil*: Yes.

*Initiate*: Is a manifestation of will a legal transaction?'

*Pupil*: Uhm …

*Initiate*: This has to go faster!

If recourse to the more general level is intended to solve problems for which no special rules are available, then the question arises whence the comparative surplus of meaning of the general level originates. Why should the analysis of the concept of the legal transaction unearth something that was not yet included in the rules governing specific transactions, such as a contract? This question sparked an incisive criticism of formalism on the part of representatives of the so-called 'free law movement' (see § 56). They wanted to expose the ostensible discovery of the surplus meaning, which resides in the general principle, as an intellectual trick that they called the 'method of inversion'. Instead of condensing the specific into the general, the specific is conjured out of it.

## § 43

Whether this criticism really gets to the heart of the matter depends on whether one regards conceptual systematisation as alien to the law. This may indeed have been the position of members of the free law movement. In their view, the law is manifest in local customs or legislation. When it comes to the latter, if a description of facts does not fit the wording of legislative enactments it is indicative of a gap in the law. Once there are gaps, the determination of law is legally unconstrained. Morality has the floor.

It should be noted that, by contrast, nothing scandalous happens when a property that occurs in several phenomena is singled out by the formation of a concept. As Immanuel Kant emphasised in his lectures on logic, by comparing and reflecting we discover that which is common in phenomena and pin it down conceptually.[5] It should not come as a surprise, therefore, that something new emerges as a result of conceptualisation. Whether one regards the productive force of thought as alien to the law or as immanent to it, is the question over which conceptual jurisprudence and the free law movement never agreed.

## § 44

Formalism in the sense outlined above did not only exist on the European continent, where in the German-speaking world it was closely interwoven with the so-called *science of pandectae* (the study of Roman law in the nineteenth century);[6] it also existed in the United States, where it was mainly associated with Christopher Columbus Langdell.[7]

Langdell used precedents in the classroom to provide insight into the relevance of conceptual distinctions for the elaboration of rules and principles. What he was really concerned with, however, were not the 'holdings' of court decisions, but the legal system as such and the classificatory concepts manifest in judicial rulings. He did not proceed all too differently from his colleagues in Germany, who tried to reconstruct the system of Roman private law from the short expert opinions of Roman lawyers handed down in ancient sources, particularly in the so-called *Digest*.

## § 45

Formalists take it for granted that the legal materials (ie precedents, customary law or legislation) provide the substance for the systematic elaboration of legal concepts. The concepts are supposed to elucidate the meaning of this substance (eg 'An offer is a one-sided legal transaction, so it has a binding

---

[5] A translation of Immanuel Kant's lectures on logic can be found in I Kant, *Lectures on Logic* (ed and trans JM Young, Cambridge, Cambridge University Press, 1992).

[6] See F Wieacker, *A History of Private Law in Europe* (trans T Weir, Oxford, Oxford University Press, 1995) 341–62.

[7] See, on the following, Grey, n 3.

effect') and to enable easy linkages to factual situations (eg 'Do the words and circumstances of the statement indicate that the person really wanted to engage in a binding commitment?'). Eliciting concepts from substance transforms the law into a state in which it attains greater precision than it has possessed in its original customary or statutory form. The practical benefit to be reaped from this transformation is more reliable and predictable applicability.

The legal concepts thus serve to capture the full normative significance of legal rules and to lay the foundations for the formulation of overarching principles. The latter are of greater generality than the former. As adumbrated above, principles are necessary in order to calibrate the scope of application of rules.

> *Pupil*: Negligent action is neglectful of the appropriate standard of care.
>
> *Initiate*: What is relevant for determining the appropriate standard of care? Should it be what the individual person can do or what we have reason to expect any dependable person to be capable of doing?
>
> *Pupil*: This is not easy to determine, but we will probably arrive at an answer by examining the principle of fault.
>
> *Initiate*: Good. But what is it, then, that we owe to others? Do we owe acting according to what we take to be the best of our own individual abilities or attempting to live up to the standard of a typically careful person?
>
> *Pupil*: The first alternative would leave the law to chance. That cannot be right. Hence, the principle that liability ordinarily presupposes fault requires observing an objective standard.

Formalists also consider it desirable to advance to the general level and to make explicit the forms or principles on which many legal institutions are based.

> *Initiate*: What do the state, a limited liability company and an association have in common?
>
> *Pupil*: They are legal entities.

This promises a more thorough penetration of the substance of law.

## § 46

The sublimation of the legal materials into principles and the systematic conceptual classification of the legal materials serve practical purposes. They help to avoid arbitrary decision making and render legal analysis rationally intelligible and transparent.

The legal system envisaged by formalists is comprehensive. It cannot resign itself to saying in a particular case that the matter cannot be decided.

> *Judge*: Go away! I have no clue as to how to resolve this matter and I don't even want to have one. I give a damn. *(Pauses)*. I hate you, I really do.

Even if the information for the party seeking justice is that the right she purports to have does not exist, the legal system at least has to come up with this negative answer.

Moreover, the legal system is also supposed to be complete and without gaps insofar as the answer to a legal question never has to, and must not, be made up by the authorities deciding a case. The answer must be derived from the system. It must also be unequivocal and definitive. The law cannot have more than one correct answer. There can only be one right answer.

Conceptual classifications, the reconstruction of a 'logical' pedigree in the relation between principles and rules, the reference to external facts and the abstention from moral evaluations serve to improve the applicability of law. According to its own self-conception, it does not at all arise from strange scholasticism harboured by aloof would-be scientists turning their backs on the world. Formalism is supposed to serve the 'interests of life'.

## § 47

In the German-speaking tradition, formalism places itself in the tradition of *scientia iuris*, which is considered to be of ancient origin.[8] The legal materials are taken to originate from ancient sources (and present themselves in the intellectually appealing format of opinions given by an elect group of jurists) or from contemporary laws.

---

[8] See HJ Berman, *Law and Revolution: The Formation of the Western Legal Tradition* (Cambridge, MA, Harvard University Press, 1983) 151–64.

In the area of common law, the situation is different. The common law originates from precedents. Formalism is caught in a dilemma here because of its circularity.[9] Precedents are binding if they are based on legal principles. Legal principles are binding if they are based on precedents.

The *stare decisis* principle seems to offer a way out of this circle. It invests court decisions with the authority of law. Hence, every decision that makes a difference about the law as it stands must be granted legal authority. The downside of this principle is that it seems to empower courts to change the empirical base of the system by introducing new ideas. It must be unclear, hence, whether one may ignore court decisions on the ground that they have misapplied existing law. Decisions are Janus-faced. *Ex ante* they are supposed to be applications of existing law and may hence be dismissed as irrelevant if they are wrong; but *ex post* they are also the origin of new law. They have the power to abrogate existing law.

For that reason alone, the formalist project must appear questionable in the context of common law. The authority of systematic legal knowledge in relation to court decisions must remain unclear (for further discussion see §§ 52–54).

## § 48

In continental Europe there is, however, an equivalent troublemaker, namely 'the legislator'.

According to the fundamental principles of modern criminal law, one is criminally responsible for one's own conduct or the criminal activity of others that one has aided or abetted. This is the view of modern criminal law systems. Corporate criminal law does not fit this mould. Criminal liability on the part of the company management for offences committed by employees which could not be foreseen and prevented by the managers would be absolutely 'contrary to the system'.

The notorious outrage by trained legal experts about legislation that is 'contrary to the system' is, however, not merely a vain political self-assertion on the part of a self-congratulatory elite. It reveals that law in its systematised form appears to be a *higher law* than ordinary legislative enactments. The reason lies in the promise that law *as a whole* comprises several principles within a coherent frame of reference ('under these circumstances and implied warranty, under those compensation for damages'). Systematised

---

[9] See Grey, n 3, 30.

law combines principles into a balanced scheme. It holds out the promise that the appropriate norms are applied to relevant facts and is thus capable of guaranteeing equal treatment.

§ 49

The quality of the systematically recast legal materials to ascend to the level of higher law in relation to precedents or legislative enactments points already in the direction of that formalism which may look 'wild', although in fact it is not. Its proponent, Rudolph von Jhering, presented it so exuberantly in his early work that what he had professed before would seem crazy to him later in his life.[10] Indeed, the early Jhering thought that the law is brought into a 'higher aggregate state' through systematisation, that is, through processes of 'analysis' and 'concentration'.

At its core, Jhering was concerned with the isolation of the smallest legally significant elements, which he called, never tired of using naturalistic metaphors, 'legal bodies'. Legal concepts designate these bodies.

Such bodies are either independent or dependent. They are independent when they give rise to legal effects. Dependent bodies do not do so of themselves but only in combination with others.

> *Initiate*: Give me an example of an independent legal body!
>
> *Pupil (proudly)*: An offer is an independent legal body because it binds the bidder.
>
> *Initiate*: And what would be an example of a dependent body?
>
> *Pupil*: The condition is an example of this. It can only unfold its suspensive or dissolving effect if it is attached to something that is thereby conditioned.
>
> *Initiate*: Don't use such pompous language!
>
> *Pupil*: A condition can only be part of an agreement, but never a self-standing legal transaction.

According to Jhering, the transformation of the legal materials into elements requires a certain artistic ingenuity. Once this task has been accomplished,

---

[10] Jhering's ideas, from which he later recoiled, can be found in R von Jhering, *Der Geist des römischen Rechts auf den verschiedenen Stufen seiner Entwicklung*, vol 1, 6th edn (Leipzig, Breitkopf und Härtel, 1907); vol 2/2, 5th edn (Leipzig, Breitkopf und Härtel, 1898). I develop my interpretation of Jhering's ideas in 'Legal Formality and Freedom of Choice: A Moral Perspective on Jhering's Constructivism' (2002) 15 *Ratio Juris* 52–62, and in my book *Rechtssystem und Republik: Über die politische Funktion des systematischen Rechtsdenkens* (Vienna, Springer, 1992).

legal analysis ascends from the netherworld of the interpretation of statutes to the heights of constructivist legal scholarship. The law is thereby given an altogether different appearance. All conceivable legal consequences are packed into the composition of bodies. The right of ownership means that a thing can be used at will, freely sold, and, in the event of damage, it is transformed into a claim for damages against a tortfeasor. Evidently, several legal rules have to be 'condensed' for the purpose of constructing bodies.

Once law has been brought into the higher aggregate state, it takes on a form in which the generation, modification and disappearance of legal bodies by virtue of actions and events can be accounted for as though these were natural phenomena. Linking descriptions of facts to conditions established by a norm is no longer necessary, especially as the law in the form of the legal body wipes off its prescriptive mood. It presents itself as if legal effects were triggered by causes ('If a marriage is irredeemably shattered it is ready for divorce'). The legal consequences of the use of the legal body can thus be read off its face.

> *Initiate*: A house protected by fire insurance burns down. What does this mean, legally speaking?
>
> *Pupil*: Due to the fire, the destroyed part of the property is transformed into a claim to receive benefits from the insurance company.
>
> *Initiate*: When will this happen?
>
> *Pupil*: Within a split second; or: a 'logical second' as the Germans would have it.

The law, reduced to its legal elementary particles, also contains the grammar of legal life. This grammar indicates which bodies can emerge from others and how they can be combined.

> *Initiate*: Can you be bought?
>
> *Pupil*: No, because being a person cannot be combined with a sales contract.
>
> *Initiate*: In other words, the sale of a person cannot be legally articulated.

The focus rests on clarifying how obligations and rights can be created, altered or eliminated through the behaviour of parties, uninvolved persons or natural events. By analogy with Saussure's distinction between language as a system of rules (*langue*) and as a practice of communication (*parole*), it can be said that law is realised in legal relationships in the same way that language (*langue*) is realised in speech (*parole*) and in texts.[11]

Reading the world through the lens of the elements makes the adjudication of legal issues relatively simple. According to Jhering, legal knowledge has already provided us with this service for centuries. He merely elaborates in pictorial language how we proceed when we analyse legal problems. We begin with a legal body in its initial state and examine whether and to what extent is has been modified through the course of events.

In this respect, we are still formalists today.

§ 50

Jhering's idea of transforming the legal materials that we encounter in the form of imperatives or social rules into legal bodies must nevertheless appear strange and peculiar. Conceiving of the legal analysis of facts as observing the emergence and alteration of legal bodies is too reminiscent of the natural sciences. Knowledge of the law, however, does not deal in causal explanations. It says what ought to be done or what can be done with what legal effect.

Indeed, assimilating legal scholarship to 'science' in a scientific sense is misleading. But that has never been the intention of those professing *scientia iuris*. It has always been supposed to designate the style of knowing the law that is *appropriate* to the object of this knowledge. The knowledge of the law must be compatible with the law itself. And this adequacy and compatibility are based in no small part on facilitating an easy application of the law to the facts.

§ 51

This intrinsic connection between the form of knowing and what is known by virtue of this form becomes clear when one considers what legal knowledge is supposed to accomplish in order to live up to the rule of law.[12]

*Thinker.* The law must be general.

---

[11] See F de Saussure, *Course in General Linguistics* (trans R Harris, London, Bloomsbury, 2013).

[12] Tacitly, the text that follows draws on LL Fuller, *The Morality of Law* (New Haven, CT, Yale University Press, 1969).

Based on this premise, it is not absurd to expect legal knowledge to develop general rules from precedents by means of induction. It overcomes the randomness inherent in distinguishing between isolated 'holdings' (the objective scope of application of precedents). That must have been Langdell's concern, too.

> *Thinker*: The law must be predictable and easily applicable.

Clearly formulated rules make the application of the law more predictable than standards whose meaning remains obscure. However, the clarity of language is not a sufficient condition for the clarity of the law. In order to optimise the predictability of the law, a set of potentially applicable rules must be correlated with potentially relevant issues. Only under this condition is it possible to say which norm fits which type of circumstance. This double relation of norm to norms (which is negative) and of norms to types of fact (which is positive) is to be mediated by the system of conceptual classifications. Such a system is supposed to make legally legible what happens in real life. The readability of social facts is a prerequisite for attaching appropriate legal consequences. Only the whole package of systematic relations and classifications can give rise to something like the predictability of law.

> *Thinker*: The law must be applied equally.

This equality principle is also served by the formation of a system. If the situations are consistently linked to the appropriate legal standards, the result is the like treatment of like cases.

> *Thinker*: The law must have a correct answer to every legal question and must not allow unbridled discretion.

Legal knowledge can satisfy this condition if it can answer questions of doubt or close gaps by switching to the higher level of abstraction. The existing rules can be supplemented by having recourse to principles.

> *Pupil*: Does an employer have to give the employees adequate time for prayers?
>
> *Initiate*: Does freedom of religion also obligate private individuals?
>
> *Pupil*: Religious freedom is a fundamental right. It is a right to be free from state interference.
>
> *Initiate*: There you go!

How reliable such deductions are is, of course, another question.

*Thinker.* Law must not come under the undue influence of politics.

Legal knowledge can meet this requirement by developing a vocabulary that is politically neutral and promises to be impervious to being subordinated to a political programme.

*Thinker.* The law should not lend its voice to hollow-headed moralists.

The attempt to meet this condition is decisive for the historical gestalt of formalism. Legal questions ought to be adjudicated without regard to questions of justice. The value-free consideration of the 'nature' of the legal transaction or legal institution should do the trick. For this reason, formalists often invoked the 'essence' of a legal institution. Roman jurists, for example, were firmly convinced that the cessation of claims was impossible due to the personal character of the bond of obligation.

## § 52

In conclusion, we should return to the elementary circularity of the common law mentioned above (§ 47). It explains why the common law is not so much a legal tradition as it is an unresolved problem with a venerable legacy.

Based on what Thomas Grey calls 'classical orthodoxy',[13] a precedent can only have legal authority if it is appropriately derived from the system of legal rules and principles; on the other hand, such a system claims to rest on precedents as its foundation. How can precedents provide this basis without being derived from the system?

As we have already seen, the principle of *stare decisis* offers a way out of this circle. However, it wavers undecided between the relevance of systematically imparted legal knowledge and the affirmation of law making by means of deciding.

The principle of *stare decisis* is Janus-faced. It requires that the standard be followed that has been established in a precedent. At the same time, the decision that departs from such precedent introduces a precedent of its own. The new decision is not irrelevant, even if it is 'contrary to the system'. Such contrariety does not detract from its validity. The system is powerless. It seems to collapse with every new decision. There are only precedents

---

[13] See Grey, n 3.

and speculative discourses as to what has been encoded in them (ie their 'holdings').

## § 53

Just as in constitutional systems the legislature may repeal *post factum* any law that it deems to be unconstitutional, in the common law context it is up to the courts to identify *ex post* the precedents that they consider to be 'bad law'.

A critical perspective that merely adopts an *ex ante* perspective is not sufficient. The inconsistent decision creates new law. The legal situation after the decision is no longer the same as it had been before. However, since courts are free to identify some precedents as 'bad law', they also are free to choose the basis for fragmentary system building themselves. They thereby limit the scope of the principle of *stare decisis*.

This raises the question of whether the common law is at all possible or simply based on a misunderstanding of how it actually operates.

## § 54

The common law can only be a legal system if it is possible to identify false decisions. For this to be possible, however, it must accommodate pockets of legal science. The common law that we encounter is therefore not what it pretends to be. Some precedents are always set aside as 'anomalies' or 'bad law'. What is manifest therein is the moment of legal science that is also inherent in the common law. If it were not for this element it would be incapable of producing any legal knowledge.

However, such scholarly achievement must be authorised by preliminary decisions. The courts are in charge of the science of law. The result is trite and grey. It points to the intellectual enslavement of academic scholarship. Everyone is forced to think the way the courts think. The standard of scholarship is set by decision-making authority. No matter how absurd the premises may be, they cannot be questioned.

# American Legal Realism

## § 55

At the end of the nineteenth and the beginning of the twentieth centuries, formalism was subject to vocal and massive criticism. It is manifest in two currents of legal thought: the so-called free law movement,[1] on the one hand, and American legal realism,[2] on the other. Since American legal realism was historically more successful and is, after all, theoretically more appealing we shall focus mostly on how this movement has upended the science of law.

## § 56

The free law movement was restricted to the German-speaking countries. Its criticism of formalism was essentially predicated on two strategies.

The first strategy consisted of playing off positive law against the claims made by formalist legal scholarship. All that had to be done was to ask whether what was derived systematically from principles with the aid of the conceptual grid tallied with the legal rules laid down in a code (or Roman law sources). Such a confrontation worked usually to the detriment of formalist scholarship, for it would turn out that the artfully drawn scholarly conclusions where not at all supported by authoritative legal texts. It would appear, then, that scholarship had invented the law that it purported to have found.

---

[1] On the free law movement, see K Riebschläger, *Die Freirechtsbewegung: Zur Entwicklung einer soziologischen Rechtsschule* (Berlin, Duncker & Humblot, 1969). More recent is the contribution by S Silberg, *Hermann Ulrich Kantorowicz und die Freirechtsbewegung* (Berlin, Logos Verlag, 2005).

[2] A precursor of the realists was Oliver Wendell Holmes. His famous speech 'The Path of the Law' represents a declaration of independence of American legal theory. See OW Holmes, 'The Path of the Law' (1897) 10 *Harvard Law Review* 457–78. Steven J Burton published a superb anthology of contributions concerning this essay: *The Path of the Law and Its Influence: The Legacy of Oliver Wendell Holmes, Jr.* (Cambridge, Cambridge University Press, 2000). An anthology of selected writings by the legal realists was published under the title *American Legal Realism* by W Fisher III, M Horwitz and TA Reed (New York, Oxford University Press, 1993). The three perhaps most representative books of this movement are K Llewellyn, *The Bramble Bush: On our Law and Its Study*, 11th edn (New York, Oxford University Press, 2008); J Frank, *Law and the Modern Mind* (New York, Brentano's, 1930) and the anthology of the writings of Felix S Cohen: LK Cohen (ed), *The Legal Conscience: Selected Papers of Felix S. Cohen* (New Haven, CT, Yale University Press, 1960).

The second strategy was a modification of the first. It has been already mentioned in the previous chapter (see § 42). It consists of confronting formalists with the inversion charge. It says that through the formation of a legal system new substance is smuggled into general legal concepts that has not been part of positive law before. By deriving consequences from this substance, the law is not found, but further amended. Formalist legal reasoning was thus exposed as amounting to a fraud.

Thus, it was an essential concern of the free movement to reveal that what claims to be passive knowledge of the law is tantamount to the active creation of it. The creative impulse is merely hidden behind the smokescreen of science and thus immunised against critique.

§ 57

The most radical representative of this movement, Hermann Ulrich Kantorowicz, drew from this diagnosis a conclusion that would give the movement its name.[3] Where the law is silent even though we believe it should have spoken, there is a gap. Within this unregulated space the law may be 'found freely'. 'Free' means legally unconstrained and based on one's personal moral judgement. In fact, Kantorowicz said that the ultimate ground for free judicial law making was the personality of the judge.

Thus, his views overlapped with those of many American legal realists. The realists, however, were more radical than Kantorowicz. The legal realists perceived legitimate room for moral judgement even where there appeared to be laws or precedents.[4] The realists did not hold existing law – case law, at any rate – in high regard. This apparent lack of fidelity to law was to be criticised by Kantorowicz in his later American exile.[5]

§ 58

The free law movement had no lasting impact on German legal culture. Two reasons seem to explain this.

---

[3] See his famous pamphlet, which was published under the pen name of 'Gnaeus Flavius', 'Der Kampf um die Rechtswissenschaft' (1906), in T Würtenberger (ed), *Rechtswissenschaft und Soziologie* (Karlsruhe, C.F. Müller, 1962) 13–40.

[4] On the relationship between the free law movement and American legal realism see JE Herget and S Wallace, 'The German Free Law Movement as the Source of American Legal Realism' (1987) 73 *Virginia Law Review* 399–455.

[5] See HU Kantorowicz, 'Some Rationalism about Realism' (1934) 43 *Yale Law Journal* 1240–53.

The first goes back to the rise of Philipp Heck's *Interessenjurisprudenz* (jurisprudence of interests).[6] It provided something like a new methodological orientation after the faith in conceptual jurisprudence had been profoundly shattered. According to Heck, legislation is based on decisions that express preference for one social interest over contending – eventually defeated – others. Legislatures resolve conflicts between and among conflicting social forces through a valuation of their interests. The construction and further development of the law ought to be based on such valuations. They provide the building blocks for the 'internal system' of law, whereas the conceptual grid is relegated by Heck to the level of an 'external system' that allows one to navigate the different departments of the legal system. The evaluatively charged internal system is the site that is to inform legal decision making.

The other reason may be due to the evil example set by the jurisprudence and legal practice of National Socialism.[7] Both dissociated themselves from existing law whenever doing so was politically opportune and desirable.[8]

Apart from its moral abomination, National Socialism was a twofold intellectual catastrophe for jurisprudence in Germany and Austria. On the one hand, scholars were expelled who had what it took to produce innovative work (eg Kantorowicz); on the other hand, post-war German scholars – apart from exceptions such as Rudolf Wiethölter or Ulrich K. Preuß – often lacked the courage to deal critically with the established style of legal scholarship.[9] The fear of being exposed as advocating the erosion of the rule of law was too great.

Better keep everything under the lid.

§ 59

A happier story can be told about American legal realism, which emerged a little later than the free law movement, namely in the 1920s, even if the more radical currents of this movement soon ran into the sand. However,

---

[6] See P Heck, *Das Problem der Rechtsgewinnung – Gesetzesauslegung und Interessenjurisprudenz – Begriffsbildung und Interessenjurisprudenz* (ed R Dubischar, Bad Homburg vor der Höhe, VAS Verlag, 1968).

[7] See, most recently, H Pauer-Studer, *Justifying Injustice: Legal Theory in Nazi Germany* (Cambridge, Cambridge University Press, 2020).

[8] See M Walther, 'Hat der juristische Positivismus die deutschen Juristen im "Dritten Reich" wehrlos gemacht?' in R Dreier and W Sellert (eds), *Recht und Justiz im 'Dritten Reich'* (Frankfurt aM, Suhrkamp, 1989) 323–54.

[9] See R Wiethölter, *Rechtswissenschaft* (Frankfurt aM, Fischer, 1968); UK Preuß, *Die Internalisierung des Subjekts: Zur Kritik und Funktionsweise des subjektiven Rechts* (Frankfurt aM, Suhrkamp, 1979).

the intellectual revolution triggered by legal realism turned out to have a lasting impact. Contemporary American legal scholarship, if it is ambitious and wishes to leave a mark, must be interdisciplinary, especially with regard to social sciences, such as economics. Arguably, this is a long-term impact of legal realism.

One encounters realistic legal theories of law also in Scandinavia and Denmark.[10] Their representatives were less interested in concrete methodological questions and tried their hand at loftier pursuits, such as epistemology and ontology. In the United States, by contrast, the investment of theory in concrete issues of private and commercial law was the key to giving the realist approach broader relevance. In addition, the legal realists were strongly interested in political reform. They were opponents of laissez-faire liberalism and supporters of the New Deal initiated by Roosevelt. Some of them came to work subsequently for the government.

The main representatives of American legal realism are Walter Wheeler Cook, Felix S. Cohen, Jerome Frank, Robert Hale, Joseph C. Hutchinson, Karl Llewellyn, Underhill Moore, Herman Oliphant, Max Radin and Hessel Yntema.[11]

§ 60

How is one to conceive of a realistic legal theory of law?

The term suggests that the focus does not rest on ideal entities ('norms' or 'principles') that are to be comprehended analytically, but on causal forces (the 'real'). Straightforwardly put, a realistic theory of law wants to make us aware of how the law really works.

What is seemingly paradoxical about this approach is that the reality of the law is a double one. Reality consists of reality itself – ie the judicial

---

[10] For an introduction, see T Spaak, *A Critical Appraisal of Karl Olivecrona's Legal Philosophy* (Berlin, Springer, 2014); J Bjarup, 'The Philosophy of Scandinavian Legal Realism' (2005) 18 *Ratio Juris* 1–15. For comparisons, see GS Alexander, 'Comparing the Two Legal Realisms – American and Scandinavian' (2002) 50 *American Journal of Comparative Law* 131–74; H Pihlajamäki, 'Against Metaphysics in Law: The Historical Background of American and Scandinavian Legal Realism Compared' (2004) 52 *American Journal of Comparative Law* 469–87.

[11] The best recent interpretations of American legal realism are offered by MS Green, 'Legal Realism as a Theory of Law' (2005) 46 *William and Mary Law Review* 1915–2000, and JW Singer, 'Legal Realism Now' (1988) 76 *California Law Review* 467–544. See also RS Summers, *Instrumentalism and American Legal Theory* (Ithaca, NY, Cornell University Press, 1982); WE Rumble, *American Legal Realism* (Ithaca, NY, Cornell University Press, 1968); B Leiter, *Naturalizing Jurisprudence: Essays on American Legal Realism and Naturalism in Legal Philosophy* (Oxford, Oxford University Press, 2007). A newer introduction is offered by J Zaremby, *Legal Realism and American Law* (New York, Bloomsbury, 2014). For a rejuvenation that does not slavishly follow historical examples, see BZ Tamanaha, *A Realistic Theory of Law* (Cambridge, Cambridge University Press, 2017).

decision-making processes – *and* of the misleading representations that lawyers sustain about it (see § 12). The imaginary reality is part of reality. It is part of reality that reality becomes hidden within reality.

> *Reader*: Does it have to be so complicated?

> *Author*: Absolutely! Try a little harder.

According to a realistic view, real law consists of judicial decisions and the patterns according to which they occur. The real false representations maintained by judges and members of the profession are manifest in erroneous or empty ideas about what causes or explicates their existence. Courts believe or pretend to make decisions based on legal concepts. Such thinking or pretending is real. But it also is a mere appearance, because – at least in the eyes of the realists – the application of concepts has no rationally motivating force and cannot justify anything. Legal concepts do not provide objective reasons for decisions, they are 'nonsense'. Behind this level of appearance lurk conscious or unconscious subjective motives and social causes such as political ideology or membership in a social class. Their influence can be translated into the terms of moral judgement. Based on such a translation one can take cognisance of the true normative basis of judicial decision making.

> *Judge*: In the eyes of the constitution, the pictorial representation of sexual intercourse between humans and animals is obscene. It may be forbidden by the legislature.

> *Legal realist*: You wrongly believe that constitutional law permits banning such representations. Your aversion to sodomy reflects your petty bourgeois socialisation. Most of us are babbitts. I am not shutting myself out. But I abstain from pretending that my moral disgust is endorsed by constitutional law. It is my own.

## § 61

Felix S. Cohen used a catchy name to describe the mere appearance of a rational legal foundation and of the belief that it in fact supports something. He called it 'transcendental nonsense'.[12]

---

[12] See FS Cohen, 'Transcendental Nonsense and the Functional Approach' (1935) 35 *Columbia Law Review* 809–49. A more recent monograph focusses on his accomplishments in the field of native American law. See D Tsuk Mitchell, *Architect of Justice: Felix S. Cohen and the Founding of American Legal Pluralism* (Ithaca, NY, Cornell University Press, 2007).

According to Cohen, one encounters such nonsense in legal concepts that do not entertain a transparent relationship to either social facts or moral judgements.[13] His prime example is the idea that a corporation exists like a human being and can therefore have a 'presence' somewhere in the world. In the case of physical persons, the meaning of a person's 'residence' is something rather tangible. It refers to the place where persons live their lives (that is, where they work, live and have their family). Persons are – something that Kelsen will deny, by the way – natural facts. Corporations are not.

## § 62

*Judge*: Where is Walmart at home?

*Child*: Well, almost everywhere in the US.

*Mother*: Isn't my child right about this?

## § 63

The unmasking of the merely apparent orientation provided by legal concepts takes concrete problems as their point of departure. The question of where a corporation 'is' arises, for example, when someone desires to sue a corporation in a court of law. In which jurisdiction does the action have to be brought?

The advice given by the transcendental absurdity Cohen rebelled against was that the corporation was to be sued at the location where it 'is'. But this criterion is ostensibly empty. Corporate bodies do not sleep in beds, live in apartments or go to work.

Nevertheless, the emptiness of the presence criterion is mitigated by the fact that various criteria are considered in order to determine the location of a corporation. These include the presence of offices, one or more business premises or the subordination of branch offices in relation to the administrative hub.

> *Reader*: Here we are. There is the reference to social facts. So, the presence criterion is not as empty as Cohen pretends it to be.
>
> *Author*: I'm not finished yet. Watch out, now comes the decisive point!

---

[13] On the following see his 'Transcendental Nonsense', n 12, 824–30.

According to Cohen, courts in their jurisprudence refer intuitively and haphazardly to one 'connecting factor' and then again to another in the next case. The result is arbitrariness, which is, indeed, the negative of the rule of law.

> *Court*: The permanent renting of office space that is used for administrative purposes is an unmistakable sign that the corporation has its seat at the place where these premises are located.

When courts fall victim to transcendental nonsense, they act as if the criteria used are characteristics of social entities and that they determine the location of a corporation due to their existence: Permanent establishment of an office, a certain number of employees working on site, regular customer contact or any other factor. The 'presence' is represented as if it depended on a hodgepodge of social facts. Accordingly, the legal problem is also presented as if only a few facts need to be determined in order to solve it.

As indicated above, this expectation reflects the basic attitude of formalism. Once the facts have been established, the legal concepts apply themselves to these facts without anything further. According to Cohen, this belief is the root of the nonsense. The alleged characteristics of a social entity point to aspects the relevance of which for the resolution of conflicts needs to be judged in moral terms.

> *Legal realist*: In relation to a disappointed customer, should it matter that the corporation has rented offices? Or should it be of greater relevance that the corporation has had regular contact with customers in this jurisdiction?

The intuitive and possibly cumulative use of criteria conceals the fact that customer contact, for example, is important to protect the interests of consumers by investing them with standing at the place where they live. The seat of a corporation is nothing absolute. It is relative to the legitimate grounds of enforceability, and may again be determined differently with regard to the tax liability of a company.

If one ignores this pragmatic function of various criteria, then the talk of a 'presence' suggests that the corporation exists as if it were a thing. The truth is, however, that the existence of a corporation in a certain place should at best be an expedient to enable a reconciliation of interests between the people who use the corporation to pursue their business interests and those others who legitimately lay claims to the resources owned by these people.

§ 64

*Initiate*: The seat of a corporation is determined by where it develops most of its business activities.

*Realist*: What makes you think so?

*Initiate*: Well, this is analogous to a person's place of residence.

*Realist*: This is a reification.

*Pupil (mischievously)*: Ha-ha!

§ 65

Insufficiently structured concepts, whose properties are flexibly used to refer to legal phenomena, remain a motley assemblage. But they are not the only instances of transcendental nonsense. According to Cohen, parts of it are also circular concepts. His example of this is trademark law. During his time, the right to the exclusive use of certain words was justified by having recourse to the natural right of ownership. The idea was that whoever introduces a brand creates a value that should not be taken away from that person. Cohen pointed out, however, that the economic value would not exist if it were not for the legal protection extended to the trademark.

Semantically indefinite legal terms such as 'due process' also belong to the realm of transcendental nonsense. Owing to their use and relevance it becomes impossible to resolve legal questions on rational grounds:

> In every field of law we should find peculiar concepts which are not defined either in terms of empirical fact or in terms of ethics but which are used to answer empirical and ethical questions alike, and this bars the way to intelligent investigation of social fact and social policy.[14]

Cohen contrasts the confused discourse he encounters in court decisions with the greater transparency and rationality with which legislative bodies address issues of social policy. He is obviously convinced that the reason of law is better served in legislative processes than in contexts of adjudication. The legislature is the real seat of rational legal policy and judges would do much better if they reasoned like legislators.

*Judge*: You can't be serious, Mr. Cohen.

---

[14] Cohen, n 12, 820.

## § 66

The critique of transcendental nonsense assumes that the use of incoherent, circular or indeterminate concepts cannot be the actual basis for decisions. The relevant terms serve as mere veneer, even if the judges are unaware of this. The decisive work is done by moral ideas, whose influence is concealed by conceptual magic play. Cohen invites us to distinguish between a conscious but obscure level of conceptual reasoning that passes as 'value-neutral' and an implicit or unconscious level that is grounded in moral and political convictions.

## § 67

If different criteria are being used in a court's jurisprudence to determine the whereabouts of a corporation and if, thus, an inconsistent picture emerges, this indicates either the existence of sheer arbitrariness or that closer attention needs to be paid to different types of situations that give rise to different reactions among judges. From this follows what a realist jurisprudence has to embrace as its reconstructive task: it not only has to expose the obscuring influence of general legal concepts, it also has to find out whether and how patterns of behaviour can be made out for judicial reactions with an eye to various types of situations.

The representatives of the free law movement even celebrate such patterns as the 'living law' in contrast to the dead letter of the law or the drab and grey of the textbook. Quite a few representatives of legal realism are at home in the field of commercial law. They consider trade usages that courts accept as legally relevant as examples of patterns of such conduct.

## § 68

One of the theoretically most ambitious minds, the already mentioned Felix S. Cohen, chooses a decidedly pragmatic approach to the determination of real law. Echoing Peirce's pragmatic maxim,[15] he contends that the meaning

---

[15] Charles S Peirce first developed the pragmatic maxim in an essay called 'How to Make Our Ideas Clear', reprinted in M Cohen (ed), *Chance, Love, and Logic* (New York, Harcourt, Brace and Company, 1923) 32–60. For useful elaborations, see P Forster, *Peirce and the Threat of Nominalism* (Cambridge, Cambridge University Press, 2011) 64–79 and C Hookway, *The Pragmatic Maxim: Essays on Peirce and Pragmatism* (Oxford, Oxford University Press, 2012) 165–77.

of a concept lies in the behavioural consequences its invocation gives rise to. Ownership is therefore nothing more than the type of the assets and powers of control protected in the jurisdiction under that name.

The terminology used by realists often seems to be behaviouristic. William Underhill Moore is an example.[16] A certain type of situation is taken to serve as a 'stimulus', the court judgment is then considered to be the 'response' to it. In his scholarship, the law is therefore not presented conceptually and systematically, but with an eye to situations that are taken to be different on the ground of giving rise to different reactions by courts.[17]

§ 69

The relationship between 'stimulus' and 'response', however, can be conceived of in two ways.

For one thing, one can understand it purely causally. One event is followed by another. The regularity of the relationship can be observed, even if the existence of the causal nexus remains theoretically unaccounted for.

> *Pupil*: If you exclaim, 'police arbitrariness', the judge will decide in your favour.
>
> *Initiate*: Do you know why?
>
> *Pupil*: I have no idea. I think it's her personality.
>
> *Initiate*: What do you mean by 'personality'?
>
> *Pupil*: I don't really know. Something about her that is not something, but also not nothing.

The only regularity that can be achieved along this path is that *this* judge usually decides in *that* way. The judge's proper name denotes an opaque cause.

Of course, it does not follow from the construction of patterns that a decision ending up different from what one predicted is not a law. The view, therefore, has to embrace a decision theory of law. Jerome Frank

---

[16] See W Underhill Moore and CC Callahan, 'Law and Learning Theory: A Study in Legal Control' (1943) 53 *Yale Law Journal* 1–136.

[17] For an introduction, see JH Schlegel, 'American Legal Realism and Empirical Social Science: The Singular Case of Underhill Moore' (1980) 29 *Buffalo Law Review* 195–324.

favoured it.[18] The law is what the judge decides it is. Period. Whether the decision is consistent with a pattern of stimulus and response is just as irrelevant as whether the reasons for the decision can be made out.

This is not a terribly plausible concept of law. Not only does it put every judge in the position of a sovereign who is above the law, it reduces law to an aggregate of unrelated individual decisions. The law disintegrates into a heterogeneous mass of legal singularities.

Alternatively, the pattern of stimulus and reaction can also be conceived of in such a way that the reactions are based on programmes that are triggered by stimuli.

> *Pupil*: The judge is a lefty. If you scream out loud 'police brutality', she will decide in your favour.

The reasons for the decision are not opaque. They reflect a political attitude. The judge's behaviour is predictable. It observes extra-legal rules or is at least consistent with certain beliefs.

Many realists have defended a prediction theory of law and thereby corrected the solitary absolutism of a decision theory of law. A decision is law only if it has the potential to influence the behaviour of the judiciary in the future and to change patterns of behaviour. It will pass this threshold if it coheres with the views widely shared among members of the judiciary (at least that was the view of Walter Wheeler Cook).[19]

§ 70

The famous British legal positivist H.L.A. Hart and others have objected to the prediction theory of law, pointing out that it disregards the normative quality of law.[20] This can be realised by looking at the law from the first-person perspective of those exercising decision-making authority.

> *Judge*: I am now familiar with the facts of the case. Knowing myself a bit, I can predict that I am likely to decide in favour of the defendant.

The objection to the prediction theory says that the theory fails to recognise that legal norms are standards of conduct from which judges

---

[18] See Frank, n 2.

[19] See WW Cook, 'The Logical and Legal Bases of the Conflict of Laws' (1924) 33 *Yale Law Journal* 457–88, 476.

[20] See HLA Hart, *The Concept of Law*, 2nd edn (Oxford, Clarendon Press, 1994) 83–84.

obtain guidance. The idea that someone deciding a case is actually observing him- or herself from a third-person perspective and, in the final event, does something by doing nothing, is outright absurd. No sensible person could ever make sense of such an idea.

This objection attributes to the prediction theory an intention that it has never had. It was never conceived of as a theory of decision making. Rather, it wanted to lend expression to a view of the law that Oliver Wendell Holmes memorably described as that of a 'bad man'.[21] It is the view of someone who is merely interested in estimating the costs of his potential misconduct.

## § 71

If the law consists of the patterns of judicial behaviour and these patterns are explained on the basis of reconstructing the rules of conduct by which judges are actually guided, then a realistic theory could well regard as law those rules whose application leads to social regularity.

But the theory refrains from taking this step. This is not the case, as is often claimed, because the realists consider most of the rules to be indeterminate in content; nor is it the case because they generally assume that decisions are in fact based on purely personal factors, such as moods, illness or occupational stress. Cohen says explicitly: 'Law is not a measure of unrelated decisions nor a product of judicial bellyaches'.[22]

Rather, the legal realists do not recognise any binding force of law that would be different from the binding quality of moral obligation. That is a very important point.

> *Reader:* There comes another 'crucial point', and for me it's again going to be clear as mud!

> *Author:* Wait a second!

## § 72

One of the central questions of legal theory is whether the law, although effective, is also obligatory. What is the difference? If the law is not only

---

[21] See Holmes, n 2.
[22] See Cohen, n 12, 843.

effective, but also binding, then it should not be followed as part of the wise pursuit of one's own interests, but because it is necessary for reasons of political fairness or the consideration of the interests of others, for example.

If the law is efficacious, then its normative relevance for individual behaviour is derivative of the wisdom that one ought not to cut one's way into one's own flesh. But if the law is based on reasons that give it authority, then the law ought to be followed because the law has ordained it. Authority is exercised by having the power to tell others what they ought to do.

> *Pupil*: You must not cross the road when the traffic light is red.
>
> *Initiate*: But why? There was no car coming anyway.
>
> *Pupil*: It is nevertheless prohibited by law.

## § 73

Behind the question of whether the law has authority lurks another question. It is the question whether the authority of law is different in kind from the authority that is based on morality.[23] Morally grounded authority is mediated by good reasons for deference. In an accident situation, for example, there are good reasons to entrust a doctor who happens to be present at the scene with taking care of the injured and to follow her instructions. Probably, this is the best that can be done to rescue the injured. Thus, the moral imperative to save injured people gives rise to the doctor having authority over others.

Is the authority of law rooted in something other than morality? If that were the case, we would have found at least an explanation for the fact that the law sets aside our individual moral judgement and declares it irrelevant, unless its relevance is explicitly permitted.

> *Pupil*: The control of construction progress by a trustee systematically favours the property developer. That's wicked.
>
> *Initiate*: Like it or not, it's the law.

In the eyes of the legal realists, the law has no self-standing authority. The rules of law do not possess the authority to override our moral judgement.

---

[23] On J Raz's view of authority, see § 97.

Rather, the law is a part of morality and therefore subordinate to it. This means that the rules that explain the judicial reactions to situational stimuli compete with other potential grounds for action when it comes to practical problem solving. In other words, the application of the law is always and invariably a question of individual conscience.

> *Initiate*: But what do we then make of law that we consider to be immoral?
>
> *Realist*: We deploy all the methodological instruments offered by traditional legal reasoning to avoid morally unacceptable results. We reduce the scope of application to virtually zero of rules that seem unfair to us. If necessary, we even use the language of transcendental nonsense. Basically, we do nothing the formalists wouldn't do. We play the language game of legal analysis and are guided by our moral judgement. We trust in the accuracy of our judgement. There is nothing else that we can trust in.
>
> *Initiate*: This is a very frivolous way of dealing with the authority of law.
>
> *Realist*: Not at all, for law has only as much authority as is permitted by morality.
>
> *Initiate*: This is anarchy!
>
> *Realist*: Whatever.

This does not give carte blanche, however, for a legal 'anything goes'. Not least Cohen recognised that the legal order serves important moral objectives:

> If ethical values are inherent in all realms of human conduct, the ethical appraisal of a legal situation is not to be found in the spontaneous outpourings of a sensitive conscience unfamiliar with the social context, the background of precedent, and the practices and expectations – legal and extra-legal – which have grown up around a given type of transaction.[24]

The principles which, as we will see in a moment, Lon Fuller believes to comprise internal morality of law are not lightly thrown overboard by all realists. They are, however, regarded as moral principles among others. We shall come back to this.

---

[24] Cohen, n 12, 840.

§ 74

Fuller was not at all a representative of legal realism. Nevertheless, his observations concerning the 'internal morality' of law[25] articulate something that
even legal realists like Cohen (maybe not others) would regard as the moral
value of legality.

Fuller's idea is remarkably simple. Those who want to govern others by
means of legal rules have to observe certain morally significant principles.
Normative principles are constitutive principles. Doing the right thing gives
rise to the social phenomenon called 'law'.

Fuller describes the 'principles of legality' as the 'internal morality of
law'. While the external morality of law manifests itself in the good goals
served by law (such as justice or the common good), the internal morality
manifests itself in the way in which the goals are attained.

The principles that Fuller has in mind are all relatively plausible.

The law consists of rules and not of a collection of unbound individual
decisions. These rules are publicly known and can be known by the addressees before they engage in behaviour. Retroactive legislation may be adopted
only in exceptional cases. The rules must be clear and not contradictory
(they have to avoid also internal inconsistencies). They do not demand the
impossible and are also not changed so often that obtaining guidance from
them seems hopeless. There is no mismatch between the written rules and
their practical implementation (ie the law in action is not completely different from the law in books).

Some of these requirements would be debunked by legal realists as
naïve. They would object that no legal system could ever live up to these
ideals. But the discrepancy between ideal and reality does not undermine
Fuller's project. The internal morality of law formulates requirements of
optimisation (Fuller calls it a 'morality of aspiration'). The law can satisfy
them better or worse. What it actually accomplishes will always be a matter
of degree.

What gives unity to the principles comprising the internal morality is
the rationality of law. From this perspective, law is cast as the 'enterprise of

---

[25] The ideas of Lon Fuller mentioned in the text can be found in his work *The Morality of Law*
(New Haven, CT, Yale University Press, 1969) and are reconstructed in N Simmonds, *Law as a Moral Idea*
(Oxford, Oxford University Press, 2007), which is an excellent and particularly readable continuation of
Fuller's approach. See also K Rundle, *Forms Liberate: Reclaiming the Jurisprudence of Lon L. Fuller* (Oxford,
Hart Publishing, 2013).

subjecting human conduct to the governance of rules'. The internal morality of law constitutes the form of action whose purpose is to control human behaviour through rules.

## § 75

Viewed from one angle, respecting the internal morality of law is a matter of effectiveness, for the law will have greater capacity to control the behaviour of the addressees if it is clearly formulated and free of contradictions; but, viewed from another angle, it also serves the moral imperative of respecting the freedom of the addressees to set up their behaviour in accordance with previously announced rules and to be protected against unpleasant surprises. Nigel Simmonds expressed this point quite wonderfully:

> When a citizen lives under the rule of law, it is conceivable that the duties imposed upon him or her will be very extensive and onerous, and the interstices between these duties might leave very few options available. Yet, if the rule of law is a reality, the duties will have limits and the limits will not be dependent upon the will of any other person. Might they be dependent upon the will of a sovereign lawmaker? One needs to remember here that laws must be prospective, and must not be subject to constant change. At any one time, therefore, the law may conflict with the present will of the sovereign lawmaker. To be governed by law is to enjoy a degree of independence from the will of others.[26]

Fuller's principles of legality may seem banal at first glance. But they still have bite. In the trans- or international field one is repeatedly confronted with the question whether something that aspires to pass as a law really is law. Doubts may arise when standards are formulated in a jargon that is only accessible to initiates or when they in combination can only give rise to an indeterminate result. In both instances, a regime that is purportedly regulated confers wide discretion on bodies in charge of 'managing' certain situations. Indeed, especially in the context of crisis management, the conditions of Fuller's legality are likely to be ignored. Human behaviour is then no longer guided by rules but controlled by 'measures' that flexibly respond to situations.

---

[26] Simmonds, n 25, 101.

§ 76

Legal realists do not rule out the possibility that judges are, perhaps not exclusively, guided by rules, even if these rules are usually not derived from laws or textbooks. The observance of rules provides to a large extent the basis for predicting court behaviour.

Nevertheless, the rules deliberately applied by judges are merely *subjective* reasons. These are reasons that the judges merely consider to be decisive for their decisions. Reasons are objective, by contrast, if they are relevant to a person's conduct regardless of whether this person also considers these reasons to be relevant.

> *Reader*. Would you *please* explain this by giving an example?

> *Author*. If you think that omega–three tablets increase the fat content of your lacrymal fluid and if this is what you want to accomplish, then you have a subjective reason for taking such tablets. If you do not know that your conviction is wrong, you still have a subjective, but no objective reason for doing so. You're just imagining a causal relationship that, if it obtained, would give you reason to take these tablets.

Judges taking their profession seriously consider their subjective reasons to be objective. They will consider the rules they apply as a binding yardstick that they are not free to ignore.

> *Realist*: You know, pupil, this judge is a neoliberal. Consumers don't stand a chance.

> *Judge*: Challenges to the validity of a contractual agreement on the ground of a mistake made by the consumer are ruled out unless the mistake was caused by the entrepreneur.

> *Realist*: There, didn't I tell you?

But is the quality of reasons to appear absolute from the inside and relative from the outside – viz., the subjectivity of reasons – all there is? Is there no way to arrive at objective reasons?

According to Cohen, the external relativity of what appears internally absolute must not be the last word. In words reminiscent of Kant's *Critique of Pure Reason*, he recalls the internal connection between the explanatory

and the constructive part of the legal-realistic project and speculates about
something like a future theory of values:

> The positive task of descriptive legal science cannot ... be entirely sepa-
> rated from the task of legal criticism. The collection of social facts without
> a selective criterion of human values produces horrid wilderness and
> useless statistics. ... Legal criticism is empty without objective description
> of the causes and consequences of legal decisions. Legal description is blind
> without the guiding light of a theory of values.[27]

At the same time, the legal realists have never really gone much beyond the
incantation of the 'situation sense' or the call for an open and fair consideration of all affected interests.[28] Also, the idea that the right answer would
spring out of an empirically rich presentation of the facts, as it were, appears
to be rather strange. The realists remain essentially moral relativists, who are
aware that what may seem compelling from the inside can always look relative from the outside.[29]

§ 77

The legal positivist H.L.A. Hart scolded the legal realists for reducing the
normative function of rules to something factual.

Surprisingly, however, Hart, as a legal positivist, was closer to the realists
than he thought.

Hart held the view that the normativity of social rules – including the
social convention based on which applicable law is identified – is rooted in
convergent behaviour that is accompanied by critical attention paid to deviant behaviour.[30] Everyone is doing the same thing, and everyone is keen on
seeing everyone else doing that too.

> *Pupil*: Imagine, I went into a church, and everyone looked at me so
> sternly until I realised that I had forgotten to take my hat off. That
> was embarrassing.

> *Initiate*: Yes, yes, you have got to take your hat off in church.

---

[27] Cohen, n 12, 849.

[28] See, with an eye to Llewellyn, W Twining, *Karl Llewellyn and the Realist Movement* (London,
Weidenfeld & Nicolson, 1973, reprint 1985) 218–27.

[29] On the Realists' failure to come up with a sound moral theory, see L Kalman, *Legal Realism at Yale,
1927–1960* (Chapel Hill, NC, University of North Carolina Press, 1986). On Cohen's attempt to arrive
at a moral theory of legal criticism, see FS Cohen, *Ethical Systems and Legal Ideals: An Essay on the Foundation of Legal Criticism* (New York, Falcon Press, 1933).

[30] See Hart, n 20, 88–90, 99, 102–03.

The normativity of the rule – that is, what distinguishes it from a factual pattern of behaviour – resides in the critical attitude with which people observe whether others are committing a mistake or deviating from the norm. This attitude is manifest and expressed in statements such as 'Now you have to' or 'But you should have'.

But what does the critical attitude use as its standard of reference? It cannot be anything else than the convergent behaviour itself. What a *social* rule stipulates can by definition only be manifest in behaviour. Convergence indicates that everyone is on the same page.[31] If it were not grasped intuitively, the rule would not amount to what it is claimed to be, namely a rule.

> *Initiate*: In church, *one* has to take one's hat off.
>
> *Reader*: Great how you do it with the *italics*. I can almost hear him say that.
>
> *Author*: Me too! And I'm even a little scared.

Should convergence no longer come to pass, the rule disappears. In order to exercise social power, the critical attitude therefore has to be backed up by converging behaviour and be capable of reliably predicting it. The normativity of a social rule is rooted in anticipating what is inevitably going to happen. Its backbone is future conduct against which deviation is unable to establish an alternative rule or to abrogate it altogether.

The performative force of the critical attitude rests on anticipating a future that is unmoved by criticisms or objections.

But if that future is different, the normative force of the rule becomes drained of its effect and thus empty. The critical attitude is then only suitable to provide refuge and shelter to the 'weirdos' who do not get it that things have already changed.

> *The mad human (holding a lantern in his left hand, his baseball cap in his right) plunges into a church where all men are wearing hats*: What is wrong with you? You have to take your hat off in church. *The priest gestures towards the sacristan and a few altar boys to remove the insane man from the church. The insane man continues walking towards the altar and shouts*: Hats! Hats! And I seek God! Am I the only one still looking for God?[32]

---

[31] See, on 'regularism', RB Brandom, *Making it Explicit: Reasoning, Representing, and Discursive Commitment* (Cambridge, MA, Harvard University Press, 1994) 27–28.

[32] The 'mad human' (or 'insane man') is Nietzsche's *Toller Mensch* from *Die Fröhliche Wissenschaft*. See F Nietzsche, *The Gay Science* (trans J Naukhoff, Cambridge, Cambridge University Press, 2001).

If there is no convergence, the normativity inherent in the critical attitude is undermined by facts.

It is not the case, however, that the critical attitude demands convergence. This is not its point of reference, for it would be only the consequence of its application. The critical attitude requires observance.

## § 78

Gustav Radbruch provided us with another concession to the realistic view of legal knowledge when he coined the concept of 'legislative injustice' in a retrospective assessment of certain aspects of law under National Socialism.[33] In so doing, he anchored the validity of the law extensively in moral considerations.

According to Radbruch, positive laws fulfil an important function. By virtue of their sheer existence they hold out the promise of legal certainty. If laws are in place, we can have a sense of what authority expects us to do.

Legal certainty, however, is not the only value that is served by the law. The law must also be just. The core of justice, according to Radbruch, is equality.

If everyone could deny laws' validity because they seem unfair to them based on their individual moral convictions, legal certainty would be close to nil. There could be no such thing as positive law. Radbruch concludes from this that legal certainty must take precedence over justice. We must put up with laws even if they strike us as unjust.

This priority of legal certainty comes to an end, however, when the law is gravely or horrendously unjust. Then the law can no longer redeem its claim to validity by having recourse to legal certainty.

The circumstances under which the law does not apply because of the injustice it contains have been expressed in two ways. Robert Alexy has

---

[33] Gustav Radbruch's ideas of legal philosophy can be studied in an outstanding edition of his *Legal Philosophy*: G Radbruch, *Rechtsphilosophie: Studienausgabe*, 2nd edn (ed R Dreier and SL Paulson, Heidelberg, C.F. Müller, 2003). For a further elaboration, see R Alexy, *Mauerschützen: Zum Verhältnis von Recht, Moral und Strafbarkeit* (Göttingen, Vandenhoeck & Ruprecht, 1997). Parts of Radbuch's work have been translated into English: *The Legal Philosophies of Lask, Radbruch, and Dabin* (ed EW Patterson, trans K Wilk, Cambridge, MA, Harvard University Press, 1950).

described them as the 'intolerability formula' and the 'denial formula'.[34] Both are clearly expressed in the quote from Radbruch below:

> The conflict between justice and legal certainty may well be resolved in this way: The positive law, secured by legislation and power, takes precedence even when its content is unjust and fails to benefit the people, unless the conflict between statute and justice reaches such an intolerable degree that the statute, as 'flawed law', must yield to justice. It is impossible to draw a sharper line between cases of statutory lawlessness and statutes that are valid despite their flaws. One line of distinction, however, can be drawn with utmost clarity: Where there is not even an attempt at justice, where equality, the core of justice, is deliberately betrayed in the issuance of positive law, then the statute is not merely 'flawed law', it lacks completely the very nature of law. For law, including positive law, cannot be otherwise defined than as a system and an institution whose very meaning is to serve justice.[35]

The 'denial formula' is very pellucid in cases where certain groups of people are treated as 'subhumans'.

Since it depends on the degree of injustice in relation to legal certainty, the determination of legal injustice involves an act of balancing.

---

[34] See R Alexy, *The Argument from Injustice: A Reply to Legal Positivism* (trans B Litschewski Paulson and SL Paulson, Oxford, Oxford University Press, 2010).
[35] G Radbruch, 'Legislative Injustice and Supra-Statutory Law' (1946), trans B Litschewski Paulson and SL Paulson, (2006) 26 *Oxford Journal of Legal Studies* 1–11, 7.

# Modern Legal Positivism

## § 79

*An underpass in front of the Palace of Justice. The judge lights a cigarette. The initiate grimaces in disgust and steps back a little.*

> *Judge*: What are we going to do now?
>
> *Initiate*: I am not quite sure yet. Maybe we just put our cards on the table and say that the law allows us all that. It gives us the power. *Breathes in through his nose and repeats between his teeth*: The Power!
>
> *Judge*: That's damn risky.

## § 80

No matter how one looks at it, American legal realism turns out to be an extremely plausible legal theory. We provide accounts of our own actions and those of others in the language of morality. We justify what we do or do not do to ourselves and to others by saying, 'We couldn't help but …' or 'It's up to us whether …'. In the context of planning our actions, the legal system influences a number of important accompanying circumstances. Of course, all that we are ordinarily interested in when we take the law into account is the probable reactions that we might get from the authorities. We want to be able to anticipate them. But even as adjudicating legal officials we would not simply drop moral considerations. We would perceive the law's claim to validity against their background. If we attach greater importance to legal certainty and put aside our own substantive moral judgement, then we do so for reasons of our own political morality (and possibly also occasionally out of opportunism). Such action is in principle fully compatible with morality – for example, holding the office of a judge with the aim to make the world a better place.

It should come as no surprise to us that savvy laymen and lawyers alike often reason comparably to American legal realists. It is the most natural thing to do.

## § 81

This makes it all the more difficult to understand why law students are not told from the very first day of class that they are being trained into a special and somewhat peculiar way of writing and talking; that this training is a remnant of another age; that they should make the best of it by using their analytical skills and listening to the voice of their conscience; and that they could learn the really exciting things about law from the social sciences. What would be the danger or harm of an open commitment to legal realism?

*Judge*: Well, that's all I need!

Indeed, judges or professors of law would act out of character if they declared that all legal speaking was of dubious intellectual merit and that individual morality was all that really mattered.

*Reader*: But why?

For judges, the personal responsibility would become unbearably onerous. They would have to admit openly that what is commonly referred to as their 'worldview' determines how they go about exercising their office. This is difficult to reconcile with sustaining their impartial and exalted demeanour. It would only be compatible with it if it could be shown that the influence of such a world view is unavoidable. Subtle explanations would have to be found for such inevitability. It is, however, not to be expected that subtlety can be easily communicated to the public without running into difficulties.

*Convict (to the judge)*: You Nazi swine!

Professors of law, in turn, would be deprived of a means of earning sizable income if their expert opinions lacked the requisite aura of technocratic neutrality. One could no longer take it for granted that it is the law itself that speaks in their long statements. It would be obvious that either their personal point of view or the client's interests determine their expertise.

*Initiate*: I forbid any intimations that my science is for sale!

*Author*: But there was no mention of that.

*(The child begins to cry)*.

§ 82

These are not the only reasons that make it inappropriate for the torchbearers of legal knowledge – the judges and professors – to admit openly an allegiance to legal realism. There are at least two others, which also explain the importance of the modern legal positivist project.[1]

The first reason is that the law, at any rate de facto, claims to take precedence over moral judgement. This means that positive law recognises the relevance of moral judgement only to the extent that such recognition is permitted by the law itself. It is a remarkable fact about law that law *actively* draws a line vis-à-vis morality.

If there is something to the law's superior claim to authority, then the prospects for a realist jurisprudence look grim.

Yet, there is little reason to worry that we must abandon realism quickly. It is not to be expected that the law's claim to authority can ever be entirely independent from the moral domain. From this angle, it is scarcely possible to rebut legal realism.

The second reason is related to the first, even if it does not directly follow from it. The prediction theory of law cannot explain why normative relevance is attributed to positive law itself when it comes to asserting and substantiating claims to legal validity. In a court of law, an argument must appeal to, or demonstrate, what 'the law' requires. It is true that attorneys signal in briefs to lower courts how higher courts have decided the issues and in this respect their arguments may be impregnated with predictions; but at least before the highest court – and not only before that court – one must refer to what the law says. Appeals to precedents of this court presuppose for their normative relevance the principle of equal treatment, by which the highest court is also considered to be bound.

Modern legal positivists have concluded from this that from the 'internal perspective' of those who produce legal knowledge the law is a binding standard of conduct and not merely an empirical pattern of behaviour. This internal normativity of law has been debunked by legal realists owing to a blanket suspicion of absurdity. The modern legal positivists charge the realists with having thrown the baby out with the bathwater and defend the relevance of this 'internal perspective' of the legal system. After all, in their view it is part of the social phenomenon that even legal realists claim to study.

---

[1] A basic text of modern legal positivism is certainly HLA Hart, 'Positivism and the Separation of Law and Morals' (1958) 71 *Harvard Law Review* 593–621.

§ 83

Modern legal positivism, however, is ready to make a significant concession.

Earlier legal positivists, such as Karl Bergbohm in Germany or John Austin in England,[2] had not yet perceived the problem of formalism diagnosed by legal realism. They merely wanted to clarify the social conditions under which legal systems are possible. The problem of building conceptual castles in the sky was unfamiliar to them. A noteworthy exception was Jeremy Bentham,[3] who was at least critical of the common law ideology of his time. But aside from him, English jurisprudence, at any rate, did not address formalism or conceptual jurisprudence as a problem.

Hans Kelsen's modern legal positivism — and this is the distinguishing mark of this type of positivism — contributes to the criticism of contemporary jurisprudence.[4] Even though entirely unaware of what is going on across the Atlantic, he is largely in agreement with legal realism about the critical programme. In fact, historically Kelsen is even ahead of the realists. Kelsen's critical edifice is almost finished when the American realists begin.

In many respects, his internally modified version of legal positivism almost seems like a contribution to a realistic project. For example, the American legal realist Robert Hale attempted to demonstrate that private legal relations constitute anything but a sphere that is free of coercion.[5] Rather, private law creates the contextual conditions under which one is put in a position to force the other to behave in certain ways. In an analytically less complex but comparatively more direct way, Kelsen rejects the

---

[2] See K Bergbohm, *Jurisprudenz und Rechtsphilosophie*, vol 1 (Leipzig, Duncker & Humblot, 1892); J Austin, *The Province of Jurisprudence Determined* (ed W Rumble, Cambridge, Cambridge University Press, 1995).

[3] On Bentham, see the magisterial study by GJ Postema, *Bentham and the Common Law Tradition* (Oxford, Clarendon Press, 1986).

[4] Hans Kelsen's oeuvre is extensive and excruciatingly repetitive. I only mention the two editions of *Reine Rechtslehre* (Leipzig, Deuticke 1934, and Vienna, Deuticke, 1960, respectively) and the *Allgemeine Theorie der Normen* (Vienna, Manz, 1979, published posthumously by R Walter and K Ringhofer). There exist English translations of all three works: *Introduction to the Problems of Legal Theory* (trans B Litschewski Paulson and SL Paulson, Oxford, Clarendon Press, 1992); *Pure Theory of Law*, 2nd edn (trans M Knight, Berkeley, CA, University of California Press, 1967); *General Theory of Norms* (trans M Hartney, Oxford, Clarendon Press, 1991). In this last work, the pure theory is already dismantled. To start with, I recommend the first edition of *Reine Rechtslehre*, possibly the new edition prepared by M Jestaedt (Tübingen, Mohr, 2008). On the different periods of Kelsen's work see SL Paulson, 'Arriving at a Defensible Periodization of Hans Kelsen's Legal Theory' (1999) 19 *Oxford Journal of Legal Studies* 351–64. A comprehensive biography of Kelsen's life and work has recently been published by T Olechowski, *Hans Kelsen: Biographie eines Rechtswissenschaftlers* (Tübingen, Mohr, 2020).

[5] Robert Hale's views on mutual coercion can be found in RL Hale, 'Coercion and Distribution in a Supposedly Non-Coercive State' (1923) 38 *Political Science Quarterly* 470–94.

distinction between public and private law as ideologically motivated and fictitious. Public law is often described as the area of law in which the organs of the state issue commands, and others, those 'subject to the law', have to obey. By contrast, private law, so the story goes, does not recognise superiority and subordination, but only horizontal dealings among equals. Kelsen rejects this contrast. Employers give orders to employees, and likewise does a creditor who claims the debt that is owed to her. Wherever there is a law someone determines at some point what ought to be done by another. In this respect all law is 'public law'.

But Kelsen also tackles other 'dualisms,' such as that of the state and law. The state theory of his time assumed that the state preceded law logically and that law was the state's creature. Kelsen undertakes to prove that the state cannot be imagined without law and that in the end the state and the law are the 'same'. He attacks the distinction between natural persons and artificially created 'legal persons' (such as corporations) by stating that the natural person is also a creation of law. The natural person is nothing natural at all, but a bundling of rights and obligations, a 'sublegal order' within the legal system. Kelsen makes various attempts to expose as deceptive the dualism between domestic law and international law. In reality, there can be only one global legal system. Kelsen rejects the idea that subjective rights – such as the rights we are born with – may exist without these being constituted by objective legal rules. No subjective right without objective law. Like the legal realists, Kelsen believes that interpreters of law are free to choose any of the so-called methods of interpretation to argue for desired results, because no method can claim priority over another. Like the legal realists, Kelsen does not believe that the process of law creation comes to end with legislation, but that it reaches deeply into adjudication. Like the legal realists, Kelsen is sceptical of the overconfidence of legal scholars to ascertain indisputably what the law is. Like the legal realists, he debunks as nonsense any disguising, idealising or objectifying formation of concepts.[6]

*Pupil*: Kelsen rocks!

*Realist*: He sure does.

---

[6] The works marking the milestones of Kelsen's critical project comprise, in particular, *Hauptprobleme der Staatsrechtslehre entwickelt aus der Lehre vom Rechtssatz, Werke* vol 2.1 (ed M Jestaedt, Tübingen, Mohr Siebeck, 2008); *Das Problem der Souveränität und die Theorie des Völkerrechts: Beitrag zu einer reinen Rechtslehre* (Tübingen, Mohr, 1920); *Der soziologische und der juristische Staatsbegriff: Kritische Untersuchungen des Verhältnisses von Staat und Recht* (Tübingen, Mohr, 1922); *Allgemeine Staatslehre* (originally published 1925, ed M Jestaedt, Tübingen, Mohr, 2019). This work is available in revised form in English as *General Theory of Law and State* (originally published 1945, ed AJ Treviño, London, Routledge, 2005).

§ 84

Kelsen's position on the problem of interpretation is key to understanding his whole theory.[7] Legal positivists typically consider the interpretation of legal provisions to be the actual anchor of legal knowledge. Kelsen's approach is no different, with one exception. He believes that one cannot say that one method of interpretation is preferable to another. From a legal perspective, any method may be chosen.

This view is not the upshot of exaggerated scepticism. Understanding speech is an art. Judgement is required in order to determine whether an utterance has to be understood literally or whether it has to be interpreted in light of the context in which an utterance has been made.

> *Municipal ordinance*: The consumption and carrying of alcohol is prohibited in pedestrian zones.

> *Thinker*: May I carry a bottle of wine in a shopping bag through the pedestrian zone?

> *Initiate*: If you interpret the norm literally, this behaviour falls within the scope of the prohibition ('carrying'). However, it was issued with the aim of preventing raucous alcoholic conviviality. Thus understood, the verbal sweep of the ordinance has to be teleologically restrained. Its use must be limited to carrying alcohol with you with the clear intent of consuming it in the pedestrian zone (for example by carrying an open can of beer or an open bottle of wine).

> *Pupil*: Which interpretation must be chosen?

> *Initiate*: According to Kelsen, the body applying the law may legitimately choose one or the other interpretation.

> *Pupil*: May political ideology influence this choice?

> *Thinker*: Why shouldn't it?

> *Thinker*: If this Nazi swine of a judge wanted to punish me because I'm carrying my Chateau Margaux in a briefcase through the pedestrian zone, could she really do so?

---

[7] See, for example, Kelsen, *Introduction*, n 4, 77–89.

*Pupil*: Yes, she could.

*Reader*: But that's the same as with the legal realists!

*Author*: Yes, with one important difference. The politically motivated decision must be articulated by using an interpretation method.

From Kelsen's agnosticism with regard to methods of interpretation follows a creative element that inevitably trickles into the application of the law. The applicable legal norm does not determine its own interpretation. Rather, the choice of the interpretation method determines how the norm is prepared for its application. Only the 'frame' of possible interpretations sets a limit to this creative process. But this framework is notoriously wide, for it is generated also by the type of teleological interpretation that permits the interpreter to divine the purpose from the broader social context of a law. Almost any construction is possible then.

§ 85

At this point something comes to the fore that could be described as Kelsen's 'basic operation'. Wherever knowledge of the law does not yield a clear result, it must be assumed – in order to make the application of law nevertheless possible – that the body applying the law has the legal power to determine the indeterminate law. Uncertain legal terms are consequently understood to be minute power-conferring rules that empower adjudicating bodies to attribute meaning to them on a case-by-case basis. The scepticism regarding the reach of legal knowledge is thus transformed into authorisations to make binding choices.

*Pupil*: What does the concept 'human dignity' mean?

*Reader*: According to Kelsen, it has the meaning that the courts attach to it.

*Jerome Frank (looking down from the sky between the clouds)*: Hey folks, this reminds me of my claim that an earlier judicial decision means what the later judge says it means. That Kelsen is one hell of a guy![8]

*Initiate (with a strong German accent)*: Did Kelsen really mean it that way? *(to the pupil)* Discuss!

---

[8] J Frank, *Law and the Modern Mind*, 2nd edn (New York, Brentano's, 1931) 149 (footnote).

## § 86

Kelsen is a representative of legal positivism, nonetheless. In his view, the creation of all law presupposes social facts that can be described in value-neutral terms (as behaviour or speech). Once the law has seen the light of day, it is there. The being of law – its validity – does not imply that it is sufficiently determinate for the purpose of application to each case. But it is so far determined that it can be referred to in sentences of empirical legal science.

The value-neutral description of positive law is the task of legal knowledge. According to the classical legal positivist's view, a clear dividing line to morality must be sustained for the purpose of description. H.L.A. Hart has expressed this 'separability thesis' such that it is one thing to describe the law as it is and another to think about how it ought to be.[9]

Even before Kelsen, it was the trademark of legal positivism to consider social facts as decisive for the emergence of current law and to sever the description of positive law from its moral evaluation. Kelsen moves beyond this by integrating the criticism of formalism into legal positivism.

## § 87

What distinguishes Kelsen from the legal realists, however, is his conviction that the law cannot be reduced to an aggregate of patterns of behaviour. As a result of such a reduction, what constitutes the law would be lost. The difference from realism is clear. The law is not made up of facts. It is made of norms.

Nevertheless, it is useful to make Kelsen's theory intelligible with an eye to an alternative legal-realistic approach, namely the decision theory of law (see § 69). In the previous chapter, we ended up rejecting that theory as implausible. Kelsen's theory supplies the element that makes the decision theory seem more plausible. But before we return to that (see § 93) we have to understand why Kelsen insists on the normative quality of law.

## § 88

According to Kelsen, the inevitability of the normative is the result of a simple observation. The law does not belong to the world of natural facts. It is linked to social facts without being one itself.

---

[9] See Hart, n 1.

Natural facts are the silent monuments of mechanically operating nature. The stone has fallen to the ground. Gravity has done its work. Nature is made to speak with the means of mathematics.

Social facts, on the other hand, appear in an interpreted state or in a state bearing the mark of an interpretation.[10]

> *Pupil (pointing at the initiate)*: This is the Professor.
>
> *Mother*: You can't really tell by looking at him.
>
> *(The child cries strongly.)*

Social facts are incidents and facts that are already cast in a certain light. The light that falls on them arises from interpretations. These are partly based on the application of norms.

> *Initiate*: What do you call it when people use money that others have entrusted to them for their own benefit?
>
> *Pupil*: We call this 'embezzlement.'
>
> *Initiate*: How do we know that?
>
> *Pupil*: From the provision of the penal code that makes such conduct punishable.

According to Kelsen, norms function as 'interpretative schemes'. They lend a certain significance to an occurrence or state of affairs. The facts take on this significance with a view to a possible legal consequence by creating a generally relevant social fact, such as an 'institutional fact'. 'Marriage' would not exist without norms that constitute marriage as a social fact.

> *Initiate*: In Louisiana, African Americans were regularly lynched, even if only on the ground of an allegation that they had taken advantage of a white woman. No one doubted that African Americans had deserved this. How do you interpret that legally?
>
> *Pupil*: As an egregious injustice.
>
> *Initiate*: Rubbish! Lynching was customary law, hence a recurring usage that was supported by the understanding that the usage is sustained as a matter of right.
>
> *Author*: This is an extremely tasteless example, shame on you.
>
> *Initiate*: Oh, stay out of this!

[10] See Kelsen, *Introduction*, n 4, 9–15.

Perceiving something as an expression or in light of norms – for example, as fulfilling the conditions for the existence of customary law – means seeing it as an expression of something else. There is always an *elementary idealisation* built into this. A complex fact is simplified and viewed as an expression of a concept. To interpret conduct as 'embezzlement' idealises this conduct insofar as it is seen as an example of an ideal content that can be regarded as fully or only inadequately realised. The interpretation carries the meaning of the concept into the factual description. The idea touches the material. It 'idealises'.

One comes across *pronounced idealisations* when the meaning of an idealisation or the normative consequence that is attached to it is presented as desirable or good. They are to be met with caution or even suspicion, especially when the idealisation is brought about by legal norms themselves.

> *Article 10(1) of the Treaty on European Union*: The functioning of the Union shall be founded on representative democracy.

This norm suggests, at least, that the Union, when it is actually working, works like a representative democracy.

## § 89

Only in the case of constitutive rules that serve the purpose of constructing an institutional fact (a 'status', such as that of being married) is the function of the norm exhausted in creating an idealisation. In other cases, the idealisation is simply its by-product. Legal norms are linked to idealised factual situations. The behaviour that is to be *interpreted* as 'embezzlement' is to be punished. The behaviour that is to be interpreted as the 'conclusion of a contract' is taken to create a new legal standard that applies to the conduct of the contracting parties.

Idealisations are not always correct. They can be false. Pronounced idealisations can serve to deceive or at least palliate something by making it look better or more significant than it really is. Every well-prepared tax return is replete with idealisations of this kind. The Captain of Köpenick impersonated a military commander so skilfully that everyone believed that he actually was in command. The exercise of authority is constituted by norms that confer power, and once this is done the deportment of those holding an office signals to others who they are. In the case of the Captain of Köpenick, the idealisation was wrong. The man created an appearance, even though an essential condition for the existence of the command authority was missing, namely the appointment as a captain.

## § 90

Three different mistakes can be made in an idealisation of facts.

The first mistake is to carry it out, although the factual conditions that permit the idealisation are absent or doubtful. This may be part of a strategy because idealisations can be used specifically to dispel doubts or cover up facts.

> *European Union*: I am a representative democracy.

The second error consists in interpreting the idealising norm for the purpose of idealisation incorrectly. Kelsen is particularly interested in uncovering this error. How close his theory is to the free law movement and to realism becomes particularly apparent in this context.

Obviously, the second error can serve as a substitute for the first. Norms can be reinterpreted in order to fit facts that they actually do not fit.

> *Judge*: A common constitutional tradition of the 27 Member States of the European Union exists if the standard in question is recognised by two Member States only.

> *Initiate*: This is how the Captain of Köpenick behaves when he sits in a court of law.

The third mistake is to idealise by means of a norm that is not even valid and therefore not really a legal norm. From Kelsen's point of view, this concerns the norms of morality and natural law.

These sources of error interact. An idealising concept can be of natural law origin and lead to a reinterpretation of positive law.

> *Initiate*: Granted, our constitution does not recognise any general freedom of action. But if we consider that our constitution can only be based on respect of the freedom of the individual, then general freedom of action must be presupposed by the system of fundamental rights.

> *Realist*: There we have it. The moral judgement determines the interpretation.

> *Kelsen (from the tomb of honour)*: True, that's pompous natural law nonsense.

> (*The child is fast asleep.*)

§ 91

Owing to the attention to idealisation and its pitfalls, Kelsen's project can be understood against the background of two basic decisions.

First, Kelsen draws a sharp dividing line vis-à-vis sociology.[11] This may seem a little paradoxical, for Kelsen realises correctly that legally relevant social facts would not be what they are if they were not interpreted in light of norms. However, the demarcation concerns an explanatory version of sociology, such as that legal realist approach which rests its hope on the behavioural correlation of judicial behaviour with stimuli. In contrast to a legal theory that perceives itself as explanatory sociology, Kelsen insists that jurisprudence, precisely because it studies and carries out idealisations, must be understood as 'normology', the science of norms.

Norms themselves are not social facts for Kelsen. The medium for the interpretation of facts is not itself a fact. Although the creation of legal norms is based on social acts whose significance is captured in idealisations ('This act is considered to be an administrative injunction'), the norms themselves are ideal entities. They can be reduced neither to inner sensations that concern psychology nor to the brute facts that are of interest in natural sciences. They exist in the sphere in which thoughts exist. According to Frege,[12] Rickert and Popper,[13] this in the 'third' world of meaning (Rickert: the 'third realm'),[14] which is different from both the 'first' world of facts and the 'second' world of inner sensations.

Second, owing to the need to avoid the third error of idealisations (see § 90), the sharp line between legal knowledge and sociology needs to be complemented with another sharp line vis-à-vis natural law doctrine. Kelsen defines as such doctrine any form of legal knowledge that does not separate between law and morality. It refers to norms that are not 'posited', but supposedly amenable to rational insight alone. Kelsen's view of legal

---

[11] For the relevant pamphlet, see H Kelsen, *Über Grenzen zwischen juristischer und soziologischer Methode* (Tübingen, Mohr, 1911).

[12] The idea of meaning as residing in a 'third world' was first introduced in G Frege, 'Der Gedanke', reprinted in G Patzig (ed), *Logische Untersuchungen* (Göttingen, Vandenhoek & Ruprecht, 1966); for an English translation, see *Logical Investigations* (trans PT Geach and RH Stoothoff, New Haven, CT, Yale University Press, 1977).

[13] See KR Popper, 'Epistemology Without a Knowing Subject' (1968) 52 *Studies in Logic and the Foundations of Mathematics* 333–73.

[14] See H Rickert, 'Vom Begriff der Philosophie' (1910) 1 *Logos* 1–34. On the further career of Frege's idea see H Schnädelbach, *Philosophy in Germany 1831–1933* (Cambridge, Cambridge University Press, 1983).

knowledge, on the other hand, is predicated on the pursuit of a 'value-free' science of law.

Legal knowledge and the theory exploring its possibility should therefore neither be overlaid nor confused with matters of fact or morality. For this reason, Kelsen presents his theory under the banner of a 'pure' theory of law, which must seem rather strange to us today. But that does not matter. The strange name does not detract from the significance of the project.

§ 92

The programme is clear. As one might say, reversing Cohen, it is about recuperating transcendental sense. During a certain period of his theoretical development, which indeed includes the publication of the first edition of *The Pure Theory of Law* (1934), Kelsen presents his work in the spirit of Kant's transcendental philosophy.[15] Like Kant's epistemology, Kelsen's legal positivism is devoted to the reconstruction of the a priori – ie before all experience given – conditions under which positive law can become an object of value-free scientific descriptions. Similar to Kant, the conditions of the possibility of experience are also the conditions of the possibility of the objects of experience. Therefore, Kelsen's theory contains a conception of the legal norm and the function of the legal system. Similar to Kant, Kelsen's transcendental approach involves a strong emphasis on determining the limits that are drawn to objective knowledge. Knowledge before all experience (a priori) is possible only insofar as it concerns the conditions under which knowledge from experience is possible. No contents from beyond experience – in the case of law: what has not been laid down by someone – must be smuggled into the domain of knowledge. According to Kelsen, this means that meaningful statements can only be made about positive law and the a priori conditions governing its description.

Kelsen eliminates the moral idealisation of law as well as exaggerated expectations concerning the capacity of legal knowledge. Kelsen's rejection of the first idealisation is so radical that it affects the construction of the legal norm. As we will see below (see § 98), he understands it to

---

[15] Kelsen appears to have flirted with the 'South-West German' school of neo-Kantianism. See SL Paulson, 'The Neo-Kantian Dimension of Kelsen's Pure Theory of Law' (1992) 12 *Oxford Journal of Legal Studies* 311–32.

be a hypothetical judgement. The rejection of exaggerated expectations towards legal knowledge translates into the rejection of the 'static' unity of the legal system. This type of unity is fathomed in the idea that the entire legal system is permeated by the spirit of substantive fundamental principles, possibly suspended from the pinnacle of the 'legal idea'. The result of the departure from static unity is Kelsen's emphasis on 'legal dynamics', ie that law regulates how new law is created in the course of applying the law. Both strategies, which are critical of recognising unwarranted meanings, converge at the point at which Kelsen conceives of all legal norms as power-conferring norms.

§ 93

In the emphasis on the dynamic element Kelsen's basic operation reappears. Wherever legal knowledge cannot reach a clear result and morality must also be excluded from helping out, it can be assumed that the body applying the law has the legal power to determine originally indeterminate law in the act of 'application', which is actually an act of law creation.

But Kelsen moves beyond this basic operation in the context of reconstructing the general conditions of law creation. Interestingly, even an unlawful judicial ruling and an unconstitutional law are valid law. They are law at least on the condition that they have not yet been removed from the legal order. Ostensibly, the law permits not only the correct application of the law, but also, although only to a limited degree, its incorrect application. This is implicit in the provisions on remedies. The legislature has the legal power to enact constitutional *and* unconstitutional law.

> *Pupil*: The judge's opinion was simply untenable. And now the Supreme Court even confirms it!

> *Initiate*: The law itself determines which legal knowledge is sufficient to create a new law. This includes erroneous knowledge.

In this context, too, Kelsen's sober approach turns out to be fruitful. In order to understand the legal system, attention must be paid to those norms whose idealising function is necessary to reconstruct the creation of legal norms. All law creation is based on decisions that can be reversed by other decisions. Kelsen views the legal system as a concatenation of decisions. Kelsen actually differs from Frank (see § 69 and § 87) in seeing the decisions hang together. The law is not composed of isolated singularities.

Its elements are tied to one another within, and by virtue of, the social process of norm creation.

In what follows, we shall emphasise the clear separation between law and morality. This requires a small digression into British positivism and the relation of law and reasons for action. After this digression we shall be in a position to appreciate fully the radical nature of the dynamic approach (see § 101 and § 102).

§ 94

In the chapter on legal realism, the question remained open as to whether there can be an authority of law that is independent of morality. As outlined above, the legal realists had rejected such an authority (see § 76). The reasons why we consider legal norms to be authoritative are among the moral reasons for action.

Now, classic legal positivists like John Austin actually already had a good paradigm for this separate authority of the law, which is different from morality: the sovereign's command.[16]

Legal norms are orders.

Commands differ from other reasons for action in that they require compliance without regard to their substantive justification.

> *Thinker:* Close the book now!
>
> *Reader:* Why?
>
> *Thinker:* I told you to close the book!
>
> *Reader (to the author):* Well, this is a nasty crank, would you please delete him from your work?

The command must be followed because the commander has so ordered it. As a reason for action, the command is independent of its content.

~~Thinker~~

From Kelsen's point of view, the problem of command theory is that, in order to justify the authority of the law, it establishes an inferential relation from 'Is' to 'Ought', ie from a fact of sovereign power to the obligation to do as a person or institution wielding the power tell us to do. Kelsen's view

---

[16] See Austin, n 2, 22–29.

becomes understandable when one considers that according to Austin not every command is a legal norm, but only those commands that are ordered by the sovereign. The sovereign is the one who does not have to obey anyone else and whom, conversely, all others habitually obey. Obedience is explained by the sovereign's power to impose sanctions. From Kelsen's point of view, Austin infers from the fact of sovereignty that the law is binding. This is an inference from 'Is' to 'Ought'. According to Kelsen (and not only according to him), such a 'naturalistic fallacy' is inadmissible.

## § 95

Modern legal positivists have treated the command theory with neglect. This has happened because modern legal positivists have assimilated the bindingness of the law to the normativity of moral obligations. They believe that Austin proceeded like this: The sovereign has given an order. The order is considered to be law. Hence, you have a *reason* to act as you have been ordered. The reason is supposed to be of the same quality as other reasons for action. Either I carry out the order or I go home and cook for my children. The same quality of 'ought' is involved. If I do not carry out the command, I am a bad legal subject; if I do not cook for my children, I am a bad father.

Clearly, when orders are assimilated to moral reasons, the authority of orders must appear to be built on sand. Unfounded orders on the part of the ruler versus the welfare of the children: it is straightforward what has to lose out. Nevertheless, this assimilation of the bindingness of law to the bindingness of morality ignores that the relevant obligations are of a different quality because they involve different forms of coercion.

*Initiate*: What?

*Author*: Yes, coercion.

## § 96

Ideally, those who are confronted with a fact that provides a reason for action are forced to act on that reason.

*Pupil*: I think it's heroic that you jumped into the icy water to save the drowning child.

*Realist*: Don't mention it, I could not help myself.

If you asked what caused the necessitation, the answer would likely be:

>*Realist*: Nobody can stand by and just watch in such a situation.

This is consistent with how Kant explained morality as internal coercion or 'self-coercion'.[17] One's own reason forces one to act; or, putting it in the terms of empiricist moral theory, one's moral sentiments do; or, putting it more bluntly: one's fear of being haunted by feelings of guilt. This is actually the best analogy to the threats issued by the sovereign.

The necessitation by moral reasons explains, incidentally, why begging for handouts works. Beggars strategically expect good reactions from compassionate people. They are the equivalent of Holmes' 'bad man' in the field of morality (which also explains why there is something ambivalent about begging).

Austin sees the bindingness of the law as mediated by external coercion. The threat of sanctions is just as necessitating as is ideally the existence of a moral reason for action. But the threat of sanctions also coerces differently. Coming from the outside, it speaks with threats and thus supplants the voice of reason.

>*Nietzsche*: Morality is a long coercion.[18]

>*Author*: Yes, of course, just go ahead; make it even more complicated, Mr Nietzsche!

## § 97

Later British legal positivists have failed to come up with such an explanation of how law and morality differ in obligating people.

Hart considers the law to be a guiding standard of conduct, at least from the perspective of the organs applying the law.[19] He does not clarify, however, the reason for a legal obligation and ultimately gives priority to moral considerations. Whether one is to follow a law that to us seems morally reprehensible is to be judged morally.[20]

---

[17] See I Kant, *The Metaphysics of Morals* (trans M Gregor, Cambridge, Cambridge University Press, 2017). I only had the German version available: I Kant, *Die Metaphysik der Sitten*, Werkausgabe, vol 8 (ed W Weischedel, Frankfurt aM, Insel, 1968) 549–50.

[18] Nietzsche's claim that 'morality is long coercion' is to be found in F Nietzsche, *On the Genealogy of Morality*, 3rd edn (trans C Diethe, Cambridge, Cambridge University Press, 2017).

[19] See HLA Hart, *The Concept of Law*, 2nd edn (Oxford, Clarendon Press, 1994) 100–02.

[20] See Hart, n 1, 620.

Although in a manner that is much more subtle than Hart's, Joseph Raz also embeds the authority of law in morality.[21] First of all, he claims that legal norms which merely repeat the content of moral obligations have no authority different from morality. Legal norms differ from general moral precepts only if they are an outgrowth of 'practical authority'.

According to Raz, a person or institution has practical authority over me if her directives help me to do what I have moral reason to do anyway, while it is nevertheless better if I follow the judgement of authority rather than arriving at a judgement myself. Based on this view, which understands authority-based regulations as a 'service' provided to morally conscientious individuals, the law possesses authority when it is based on superior expertise or helps to solve problems of collective action. Whether someone – including the legal system – has this type of authority, however, depends exclusively on whether the directives assist in doing what one ought to do and not on an act of authorisation. In any case, according to Raz, too, the elevated position of those whose directives one follows for the reason that they have been issued by them remains rooted in morality. In his opinion, at the end of the day there is no authority independent of morality either.

## § 98

Kelsen pursues a path reminiscent of Austin, for he also wants to distinguish the authority of law – its 'ought' – from morality. He does so based on an analysis of the legal norm. In his view, the primary legal norm, correctly understood, is a 'hypothetical judgment' or a conditional.[22] Its form is that if the offence described in the antecedent condition of the norm has been committed, the legal consequence (the sanction) ought to follow:

p→Oq ('If p happens, q ought to follow')

> *Reader:* What's so original about that? This is totally unimaginative and super boring!

---

[21] Joseph Raz's theory of authority is most readily accessible in the essay 'Authority, Law, and Morality' in his *Ethics in the Public Domain: Essays in the Morality of Law and Politics*, 2nd edn (Oxford, Oxford University Press, 1995) 210–37; otherwise, it is extensively developed in his book *The Morality of Freedom* (Oxford, Clarendon Press, 1986) and defended with much nuance in *Between Authority and Interpretation: On the Theory of Law and Practical Reason* (Oxford, Oxford University Press, 2009).

[22] See Kelsen, *Introduction*, n 4, 24–25.

The wit of the construction lies in how it tacitly marks the difference to the moral obligation.

> *Supernanny (naggingly)*: Do this now! If you don't do it, you're proving to be a totally wayward person.
>
> *Newman (with a fixed stare, lifeless face, uninvolved and monotonous)*: If the condition that triggered the legal consequence has been fulfilled, then the sequence linked to it is to be realised. *(Smirks)* Whatever, nothing to get agitated about.

The primary legal norm does not even speak to the person whose conduct it regulates. Indeed, in this elementary form, it does not address itself to anyone. A legal consequence or sanction 'is to be'. This type of 'ought' is person-neutral in the strongest possible sense. No one is bound to do anything in a moral sense.

Arguably, with such a construction of the primary legal norm Kelsen wishes to indicate that the legal norm does not per se give rise to any reason for action. He thereby offers an alternative to Austin's command theory. Nevertheless, he also goes beyond Austin's differentiation of legal and moral obligation. In Austin, the element of coercion contained in an obligation is preserved. The sovereign speaks, and all tremble with fear. This is the equivalent of the power of conscience, it merely does not speak with an inner voice, but penetrates us from outside.

> *Nietzsche wants to take the floor, but the author sees this coming and whispers sharply*: No, not now!

In comparison to Austin, Kelsen brackets the force of the 'ought' even more strongly. It thereby becomes strangely assimilated to an event triggered by natural necessity. This is betrayed by Kelsen's drawing of an analogy to causation. Just as in the case of natural laws the effect of the cause *must* follow the cause, the legal consequence *ought* to follow the commission of an offence. The first necessity is ontic, the second deontic.

> *Author (to the reader)*: By 'ontic' one means that it is about existing things, by 'deontic' that it says something about an obligation.

In the first case the consequence cannot not occur, in the second case the consequence ought to occur even if it never actually will occur. It cannot be that the consequence ought not to follow. Hence, one can even assimilate the deontic necessity to the ontic by saying that the normative necessity of a legal consequence is the necessary effect of the commission of the offence.

§ 99

The draining of the bindingness of obligations to a counterfactual 'it ought to happen' returns in Niklas Luhmann's early work.[23] According to Luhmann, expectations concerning the behaviour of others are normative when they are sustained 'counterfactually'. Even in the case of disappointment, one does not let go of them. Expectations are thus sustained indefinitely.

In the next step, however, Kelsen amends the anonymous 'it ought to happen' of the primary legal norm with the clarification that the norm speaks to the law-applying official. A violation of a legal norm by ordinary people creates an obligation on the part of some legal official to impose a sanction. Kelsen will come to recast the obligation later as an authorisation (see § 100). In any case, according to Kelsen, the folks on the ground – those ordinarily referred to as the 'norm-addressees' – are guided by a secondary norm that they construe by asking how the legal system may be relevant to their behaviour. From the perspective of Kelsen's theory, they behave like Holmes' 'bad man' (see § 70). They set up their behaviour in light of impending sanctions.

> *Poet*: By establishing a relationship between the sanction and my well-being, I am singularising myself. The 'no man shall' is replaced by my own 'I do not want'. It is my own well-being that compels me to avoid the sanction. The law reckons with this. The law is also a 'bad man'. It is a bad man expecting me to behave like another bad man.

We will discuss the ground of legal validity later (see § 104).

§ 100

There is an even stronger way of drawing the line between moral demands and the normativity of law. Over the last few years, Christoph Kletzer has reinvigorated the Pure Theory by claiming that the law consists of 'declarative sentences', as it were.[24] In his view, it is possible to reconstruct the

---

[23] See N Luhmann, *A Sociological Theory of Law* (trans E King and M Albrow, London, Routledge and Kegan Paul, 1985).

[24] See C Kletzer, 'The Germ of Law' in C Bezemek, M Potacs and A Somek (eds), *Vienna Lectures on Legal Philosophy*, vol 1 (Oxford, Hart Publishing, 2018) 1–21. See also his *The Idea of a Pure Theory of Law* (Oxford, Hart Publishing, 2018).

whole edifice of law based on statements in which the law permits the use of force.

> *Law*: It is lawful to use lethal force in order to protect one's property.

Possibly, this norm has to be complemented with another one:

> *Law*: Killing someone who has killed someone else unlawfully is lawful.
>
> *Pupil*: Since it is lawful for the property owner to use lethal force against an attacker it is unlawful to kill a property owner who has killed such an attacker.

Kletzer thus arrives at a new reconstructed legal norm. Instead of

> *Kelsen*: p→Oq ('If p happens, q ought to follow')

it reads

> *Kletzer*: p→Pq ('If p happens, q may follow')

The relevant 'secondary norm' that tells the potential thieves or robbers to abstain from taking the property of others is derivative of the impunity of self-defence.

The advantage of Kletzer's model is that it stays close to the ancient roots of law in times when it was still based on self-help. Of course, doing legal theory would not be much fun if one could not buoyantly draw counterintuitive conclusions from an elementary model. Kletzer does, and states that the permission of self-help is how the law creates peace and adds that acts of self-help are instances of law enforcement. In legal systems that rely on self-help, the state exists in a radically decentralised form.

Of course, in order to overcome the negative side-effect of such a system one has to institute centralised enforcement. According to Kletzer, this can also be brought about based on permissions.

> *Law*: Killing someone who has killed someone else lawfully is itself lawful if the first killing has occurred without being authorised by a judge.

From this follows that those taking the law into their own hands can be killed by anyone. This is back-up provided by the primary for the secondary norm that one had better refer a matter to a court of law.

Indeed, Kletzer believes that secondary norms can only emerge if the primary norms are effective in the sense that there exists capacity – force – to avenge unlawful violence with violence. The law, according to Kletzer, thus turns out to be an order of force in which the force declared lawful by the law becomes adopted as the force of law. The law itself, he says, is 'just language'. It has no power of its own. It has to be aided and abetted by the forces on the ground. The point of law is to regulate the exercise of force. From which follows that there could be no law if it were not effective. There would only be force and no law.

§ 101

What Kelsen calls the static unity of the legal system is manifest in the connection between various laws and higher-order substantive principles. Statically understood, a legal system that places the fundamental value of human dignity at its top could be viewed as comprising the conditions under which it is possible to realise this value.

As mentioned above (see § 92), Kelsen is far too sceptical of what methods of interpretation can accomplish in order to embrace such a static conception of unity. Dismissively, indeed, he states that it only has a place in morality. In the rational legal context, there is no way to trace the meaning of human dignity all the way down to the details of, say, rules governing the registration of companies. That type of unity, which Kelsen believes to be reasonably conceivable, is dynamic.

From the dynamic perspective, the legal system presents itself as composed of conditions for the creation of norms that are arranged in a sequence, ranging from the highest norms of the constitution down to the details concerning the collection of fines. At each level, these norms are validated based on decisions in which higher-level norms are both applied and creatively complemented. Kelsen believes that the more concretely the law is rendered as it passes through the stages of the constitution, legislation and court judgment, the more the emphasis shifts from law creation towards the application of law. Nevertheless, he insists that a court judgment is essentially the same as legislation owing to a like interpenetration of application and law creation.

In his later work, the two strands of sustaining the sobriety of analysis – legal dynamics and the separation of legal from moral obligation – converge. The convergence is marked by his reinterpretation of the primary legal norm ($p{\rightarrow}Oq$) as an empowering norm. Behaviour contrary to the norm engages the legal authority of whoever is in charge of imposing a legal consequence (see § 100). That this person or institution will indeed impose the sanction is to be guaranteed by another institution that is empowered to discipline the first for its failure to act. Of course, the highest organs of the system that are no longer effectively legally controlled have to be motivated to use their powers on the ground of their ambition to throw their weight around. Kelsen's approach is based on a sociological premise. The system can work only if it is driven by the irrepressible human desire to control others or to make them miserable.

> *Initiate*: Well, Kelsen lived in Vienna for a long time. He absorbed the culture.

## § 102

With that we arrive at a delightfully gloomy picture of the legal system. Above all there is the primary legal norm that does not care whether it really has an addressee or not. In order to step out of this paradoxical state in which it does not obligate anyone, it has to grow − but how? − into an empowering norm that confers on law-applying officials the authority and right to impose a sanction on those who offended against the norm. Positive law is ridden with high degrees of indeterminacy, which is brought about not least by the inevitability of interpretation. Owing to Kelsen's basic operation, this indeterminacy can be absorbed by viewing officials as empowered to lay the law down at their own discretion. The method of interpretation that they choose serves as the mere mummery of their personal morality or political ideology. The norms of positive law not only fulfil the function of implementing general norms in specific cases; they also serve to invest false applications of law with legal validity. There is no guarantee against arbitrariness. At the same time, the law cannot be 'broken' from Kelsen's dynamic point of view. Every violation of norms gives rise to the production of ever more norms. If anything deserves the high appellation of an 'iron cage', then a legal system, thus understood, certainly does.

The difference from the common law mentality could scarcely be greater. In the context of the common law, the legal system is approached with the expectation that it is imbued with community morality. It is therefore assumed that it speaks in the language of ordinary moral beliefs and that one can articulate one's concerns in a morally significant way. Kelsen's legal system is the exact opposite. It appears to be like the machinery serving a detached authority somewhere at the outskirts of an empire. It exists for civil servants only, and these are eager to keep each other in check. The law does not speak to the 'subjects'. The common people are only relevant insofar as their behaviour keeps the production of more law going.

During the period of the Habsburg Monarchy, the relationship between the imperial offices in Western Galicia and a population ignorant of the official language probably matched this picture. Kelsen's legal system is the universalisation of the colonial situation of Western Galicia into the idea of law. The law is deeply foreign, deeply arrogant and deeply susceptible to arbitrariness.

> *Poet*: Kelsen has looked deeper into the heart of the law than anyone else.
>
> *Chorus mysticum*:
>
> We study the law
>
> Not to see
>
> What we should admire
>
> But
>
> To know
>
> What we
>
> Must
>
> Be afraid of
>
> *Pupil (claps his hands enthusiastically)*: Goe-the, Goe-the, Goe-the!
>   *(The reader slaps him in the face; the light goes out with a bang)*

## § 103

Classical ('pre-modern') legal positivists explain legal validity by pointing to something factual (the de facto recognition of the legal order or the overwhelming de facto sovereignty of the commander) They do so in order to mark the difference from moral ideas. Kelsen disapproves of that. He points out that they infer something normative from something factual and thereby commit the naturalistic fallacy. From the fact that something exists it does not follow that it ought to exist.

This objection is not self-explanatory, for the point of the original legal positivist approach is to take note of the law's *factual claim* to authority. In the real world, any moral assessment of legal validity is superseded by the power of those calling the shots. Putting the matter starkly, the law is moral insensitivity fortified by violence. One should not sugar-coat this fact.

By contrast, Kelsen insists persistently that legal validity belongs to the domain of the normative. The validity of a norm can only be derived from another valid norm.

In this respect, anyone who conceives of the ground of legal validity from a moral point of view can only agree with Kelsen. But Kelsen, *qua* representative of legal positivism, wants to keep law and morality separate and, hence, to exclude moral considerations from determining the ground of legal validity.

What is it then that he wants?

His approach becomes intelligible when one takes into account that he wants to avoid two forms of reductionism.

The *limited form* of reductionism anchors the normative claims made by positive law ('though shalt not') in some fact. We encounter this limited form in modern British positivism. As we will see in the next chapter, Hart anchors the criteria for the identification of valid law in a social rule, which is something factual, but stops short of dissolving the bindingness of norms into facts, such as predictions of reactions. The factual is encountered only at the very foundation of the legal system. Once the legal system is established, it ceases to play a role.

American legal realism has already confronted us with the *comprehensive form* of reductionism. It supplants the guiding function of norms with predictions or mere descriptions of factual behaviour. If you do not do as I say, you will see what I will do to you. Oliver Wendell Holmes made this perspective famous with the following words: 'The object of our study … is prediction, the prediction of the incidence of the public force through the instrumentality of the courts'.[25] According to Kelsen, such reductionism falls entirely short of capturing the phenomenon of law.

But Kelsen is also opposed to limited reductionism. In his view, it is inconsistent to base legal validity in something factual and to regard laws as norms from which someone can obtain guidance. He believes that a limited reductionism is impossible because it would inevitably have to join forces

---

[25] OW Holmes, 'The Path of the Law' (1897) 10 *Harvard Law Review* 457–78, 457.

with its comprehensive sibling. Then, of course, the normativity of law is lost. What is legal about the law disappears.

For example, Austin's command theory anchors the bindingness of law in the superior might of higher authority, while it otherwise wishes to sustain the normative character of the commands. According to Kelsen that is impossible. One cannot have both. If the authority of law is manifest in the fact of superiority, the meaning of even a single command can only be determined by speculating about what the sovereign would *regard* as non-compliance (and whether he would take cognisance of it). What the commander de facto regards as non-compliance is decisive for what we have to take to be law. Sovereigns do not have to let themselves be told that they have to understand linguistic expressions in a certain way, for example according to standards of ordinary language. Their view counts. The imperatives are wax in their hands. It follows that the legal validity of all norms is reduced to a social fact. The normative significance of law is thereby lost. According to Kelsen, it can only be maintained if the grounds of the legal validity are also accounted for in a normative way.

## § 104

Kelsen's alternative account chooses the dynamic conception of the legal system as its point of departure. If one follows the stages model for the production of law (constitution – legislation – judicial ruling) and reconstructs the pedigree of the validity of legal norms, one eventually arrives at a historically first constitution. Whence does this constitution derive its validity? Since Kelsen wants to avoid the naturalistic fallacy and therefore does not claim that the historically first constitution enters into force de facto, he has to derive its validity from another norm. This norm, however, can no longer be a norm of positive law (if we disregard international law for a moment). Kelsen calls this norm, which has never been posited, but is merely presupposed, the basic norm (*Grundnorm*).

Kelsen has spelled out the substance of the basic norm differently at various stages of his work.[26] The most interesting formulation, however, says that a legal system is valid if it is largely efficacious.

---

[26] See SL Paulson, 'The Basic Norm Revisited' in L Duarte de Almeida, J Gardner and L Green (eds), *Kelsen Revisited: New Essays on the Pure Theory of Law* (Oxford, Oxford University Press, 2013) 42–61.

Why does Kelsen arrive at this 'magic formula of legal validity'? This can be explained with an eye to the function of the basic norm. It facilitates the transition from social to legal validity, however, without thereby committing a naturalistic fallacy.

Socially understood, norms are valid when they are in practice observed and applied. Kelsen's condition that a legal order be 'largely efficacious' refers to nothing else than to the existence of social validity. It should be borne in mind that not just haphazard patterns of behaviour are the condition of legal validity. The behaviour has to be the observance or application of norms. Such behaviour is exactly what we mean when we speak about 'social validity' or the effectiveness of an order.

Now, the condition 'largely' may sound like wishy-washy twaddle. But, indeed, it is chosen wisely and denotes the matter at an adequate level of precision. According to Kelsen, a normative order that is always and completely followed and obeyed would only exist as pretence. If no behaviour were ever classified as deviant or violative, there would be no obligation (compare this to Kant's holy will). Normativity – norms as controlling standards – would not exist socially. According to Kelsen, the same observation can be made for a normative order that is never observed by anyone. It also has no social validity. What is socially valid can only be 'largely efficacious'.

With the basic norm, Kelsen thus reconstructs the social validity of law from within its internal perspective and invests it with a norm on which it can claim to be based. Socially, again, this validity is manifest in the fact that people are guided by the norms themselves and not by predictions about how the powers that be may or may not construe these norms. Thus understood, Kelsen introduces the basic norm also in order to answer the question of how the legal knowledge of legal science is possible as a social phenomenon. And he gives this answer in a manner that is entirely consistent with legal positivism, namely with reference to the social validity of law, the meaning of which is only explicated by the basic norm. Social validity must claim to be grounded in something outside of itself.

## § 105

What is the logical status of the basic norm? Kelsen originally described it as a 'presupposition' or a 'hypothetical assumption'. But all of that smacks of an arbitrary and – shocking! – factual act. How could the validity of the law depend on legal scholars' presupposing of it?

During the most important period of his work (from the 1920s to the 1960s), Kelsen characterised the basic norm repeatedly as a 'transcendental-logical condition'.

This may seem both profound and incomprehensible. The basic idea, however, is once again plain. Legal knowledge exists, particularly in the form of legal doctrine. The latter is the social practice of legal knowledge in a context in which norms are not merely taken as indications of how judges might behave in the future. The meaning of norms is not reduced to something factual. Under what condition is that possible? It is only possible if norms are valid, which is in turn only possible owing to the basic norm. It thus functions as a condition of the possibility of legal knowledge. A condition of the possibility of experience (in this case: the 'experience' of positive law) is a 'transcendental-logical condition' from the point of view of Kant's philosophy.

> *Pupil (stooped, looking up at the reader)*: In this sense, the basic norm is 'always and already' presupposed as soon as one talks about positive law. The presupposition is not a psychological act.

Kelsen rejects his own ambitious epistemological solution to the problem of legal validity in his later work. Towards the end of his life he considers the basic norm to be 'fiction'. Adopting the philosophy of Hans Vaihinger, he describes it even as a 'real fiction'. It not only contradicts reality, it is also contradictory in itself.

The basic norm contradicts reality because it is not a norm of positive law. It does not exist. It is contradictory in itself because it gives authorisation to create law, but in order to serve this function it would have to reflect an even greater authority than the authority that it authorises.

Perhaps unwittingly, Kelsen thereby abandons his ambitious project. In the format of a self-contradictory fiction, the basic norm is transformed into an enaigmatic symbol designating the unfoundedness of law and the groundlessness of the science dedicated to its exposition.

# The Demise of Modern Legal Positivism

## § 106

The law would not exist if it could not be known. The judgment of a court could not be what it is if, in one way or another, it did not speak on behalf of the legal order. The relation of representation is established by an idealisation. The judgment of the court is *deemed* to be what it claims to be. This idealisation is the work of legal knowledge.

Modern positivism is an attempt to reduce the scope of idealisation to the extent necessary to present law as a concatenation of decisions. The ambition to render law in the least idealised way possible stems from the effort to correct exaggerated expectations concerning what legal knowledge can accomplish. Where the law remains unclear – and this may far more often be the case than doctrinalists would have us believe – the legal order is likely to invest someone with the legal power to make it clear. Powers of decision making are usually easier to determine than what substantive criteria require in individual cases. This explains why in the context of modern legal positivism empowering norms are of significant importance.

> *Judge*: Strip searches of air passengers do not violate human dignity.

> *Bernhard Schlink (offstage)*: *Curia locuta, causa finita.*

Modern legal positivism accommodates many insights of legal realism until the point at which the connection between legal knowledge and the bindingness of the law needs to be specified. Then the two strands of legal theory part company.

## § 107

In the Anglo-American world, H.L.A. Hart is considered to be the most significant representative of legal positivism in the twentieth century. He has been adopted, *post mortem*, by quite a few contemporary English-speaking legal positivists as their patriarch. Some have made it their job – up and down the world, from New Haven to Oxford – to defend the master's work against 'misinterpretations' on the part of the uninitiated. They sometimes credit Hart for having dropped those elements of Kelsen's theory that they believe to be philosophically outlandish for the simple reason that they have not originated from the milieu of Anglo-American analytic philosophy. The corresponding propensity towards intellectual xenophobia is jovially concealed in statements such as that Hart has reconciled Kelsen's approach with common sense.[1]

> *Mr. Smith (taking the pipe out of his mouth)*: You know, it's all common sense.

Hart's work is also said to have close affinities to ordinary language philosophy and to Wittgenstein's later philosophy.

> *Initiate*: Wittgenstein!
>
> *Pupil*: Ah ...

It would be injudicious, however, to affiliate Hart's work straightforwardly with modern legal positivism. In Hart's case, modern legal positivism is already in the process of being gradually dismantled, for the approach loses its critical bite in relation to the exuberant claims made by legal scholarship. The British cannot be blamed for the resultant change of outlook. They never perceived formalism as a problem, particularly since the project of legal science always remained alien to them. Not by accident, therefore, did they fail to notice that modern legal positivism was an attempt to recalibrate the function and reach of legal knowledge under conditions of substantial self-criticism. This nexus is lost in Hart's late legal positivism.

## § 108

Since Hart's work contains virtually no reflection of the reasons that stimulated modern legal positivism in the first place, its spirit is preserved only in a state of oblivion. Hart does not relate to what have been Kelsen's problems. This explains why he mocks its constructive transformation of the primary legal norm into an authorisation to impose sanctions. This doesn't seem to make *common sense*. The intellectual worlds could not be more different.

---

[1] The late positivism following Hart is manifest above all in the following works: J Coleman (ed), *Hart's Postscript. Essays on the Postscript to the Concept of Law* (Oxford, Oxford University Press, 2001); J Coleman and S Shapiro (eds), *The Oxford Handbook of Jurisprudence and Philosophy of Law* (Oxford, Oxford University Press, 2002); J Coleman, *The Practice of Principle: In Defence of a Pragmatist Approach to Legal Theory* (Oxford, Oxford University Press, 2001); KE Himma, *The Nature of Law: Philosophical Issues in Conceptual Jurisprudence and Legal Theory* (New York, Foundation Press, 2011); M Kramer, *In Defence of Legal Positivism: Law without Trimmings* (Oxford, Oxford University Press, 1999); A Marmor, *Philosophy of Law* (Princeton, NJ, Princeton University Press, 2011); J Gardner, *Law as a Leap of Faith: Essays on Law in General* (Oxford, Oxford University Press, 2012).

Kelsen suspects *common sense* to be a major source of legal-theoretical nonsense. With Hart it becomes the touchstone of truth.

§ 109

According to Hart, the law comprises a system of (primary) rules of conduct, the creation and application of which is determined by (secondary) rules of procedure.[2] Generally, he views law as a system of rules, just as if it were the equivalent of an operating manual. Legal constructivism falls by the wayside. This may explain why Hart's position on problems of interpretation is relatively unimaginative. Rules are not always clear. There is a 'core area of plain meaning' and then there is a penumbra where the meaning is more doubtful. This distinction is reminiscent of Philipp Heck's 'conceptual core' and 'conceptual halo'.[3] There is no trace of Kelsen's great insight that owing to the equivalence of interpretation methods there is an inextricable interpenetration of the application and creation of law. Likewise, Hart lacks any deeper sense of the difference between legal and moral normativity. Rather, the first is assimilated to the latter. In the event of encounters with Radbruchian catastrophes (see § 78), the law would be swiftly subordinated to morality.

When we come to Hart, legal positivism becomes wearisome. It takes its cue from the thinking of the average person and is thus whittled down to a relatively risk-free intellectual enterprise. Not by accident, Hart's theory remains quite external to the practice of law.

But this also explains why Hart's positivism enjoys great popularity. It is dignified and harmless. It does not stir up controversy nor does it disturb. Just as I don't say anything wrong when my answer to the question of who my favourite composer is that it is Mozart, as a legal academic I do not commit a faux pas if I confess allegiance to Hart.

> *The judge, the pupil and the initiate stand around in a circle and pass a Joker card among each other.*
>
> *Judge*: Hart! Ah …

---

[2] See, again, HLA Hart, *The Concept of Law*, 2nd edn (Oxford, Clarendon Press, 1994) 79–99. For a useful guide to the central themes of this work, see L Duarte de Almeida, J Edwards and A Dolcetti (eds), *Reading HLA Hart's The Concept of Law* (Oxford, Hart Publishing, 2013).

[3] Philipp Heck's distinction between 'Begriffskern' and 'Begriffshof' can be found all over his writings. See P Heck, *Das Problem der Rechtsgewinnung – Gesetzesauslegung und Interessenjurisprudenz – Begriffsbildung und Interessenjurisprudenz* (ed R Dubischar, Bad Homburg vor der Höhe, VAS Verlag, 1968).

*Pupil*: Wittgenstein! Ah …

*Initiate*: Kant! Ah …

This taming of modern legal positivism is pushed to the hilt by followers of Hart, such as Jules Coleman, who developed an 'inclusive' version of legal positivism.[4] Such inclusive positivism (see §§ 151–152) permits to the circle of legal sources arguments that aim to arrive at the morally correct answer to legal questions. The quality of such arguments to be sources may even go back to an act of legislation:

> *Legislation*: The question of who receives custody of the child must be assessed in light of moral principles.

The status of being a source of law can, however, also be conferred on morality by the social convention that is generally used to identify sources of law.

> *Common Law*: In our world, community morality is a background source of law.

Practically, on the level of the practice of legal arguments, the difference between legal positivism and its institutionalist or natural law counterpart is thereby reduced to zero.

§ 110

Of course, Hart also offers quite a few subtle analyses. In his magisterial *The Concept of Law*, first published in 1961, he develops, among other things, an alternative to Kelsen's basic norm. He calls it the 'rule of recognition'.[5]

The rule of recognition is neither a presupposed norm nor a transcendental–logical condition of legal knowledge. According to Hart, it is manifest in the conduct of the officials identifying and applying valid sources of law. They rely on the rule of recognition to recognise the norms that are normatively relevant within a legal system.

Since the rule of recognition – in this respect equivalent to the basic norm – is the ultimate rule in the hierarchical structure of the legal order, it is not derivative of another norm as far as its binding character is concerned.

---

[4] A prominent defence of 'inclusive' legal positivism can be found in J Coleman, 'Negative and Positive Positivism' (1982) *Journal of Legal Studies* 139–64.

[5] See Hart, n 2, 100–10.

But it is not 'valid'. Rather, it *exists* owing to its acceptance by the law-applying officials.

Such an acceptance does not have to involve moral approbation. What matters is that officials mutually regard this rule as the authoritative standard for the identification of applicable law. The relevance of the rule is manifest in their conduct.

> *Judge*: If we want to find out whether a decree adopted by the President is valid, we look up whether the constitution empowers him to do so.

According to Hart, it is irrelevant whether ordinary people accept the rule of recognition. In their case, all that matters is habitual obedience. So long as the officials accept the rule and 'ordinary folk' (Jules Coleman) obey even without having any 'views' on the meaning of rules, the legal system exists.

## § 111

Does not Hart infer what ought to be from what is? Hart would deny even the relevance of this question. From the internal perspective of a participant in legal discourses, the rule of recognition is used as the relevant standard. That the acceptance of this rule presents itself as a social fact from an external perspective is irrelevant for those using it internally. Drawing on it is necessary in order to make successful moves in the game called 'identification of valid law'. One can only play this game if the rule is accepted by the players, but accepting the rule is not part of the game. One merely has to be aware that it would be pointless to play the game if the acceptance could not be taken for granted.

## § 112

If one juxtaposes Kelsen's basic norm with Hart's rule of recognition, the difference could barely be greater.

> *Initiate*: Explain the difference between Kelsen's basic norm and Hart's rule of recognition!
>
> *Pupil*: But every child can do that. Child?
>
> *Child*: Kelsen's basic norm is, at least in its original formulation, an imaginary norm, while Hart's rule of recognition is a socially

practised rule. Owing to his emphasis on normativity, Kelsen focuses exclusively on the role that the rule plays inside the legal system and pushes aside as irrelevant an external description of the social fact that some social rule provides a yardstick.

*Initiate*: Well done!

If one looks more closely, one realises that Kelsen and Hart are actually saying the same thing.

*Initiate*: What?

Possibly, Hart grasps the matter more clearly than Kelsen, but he then loses sight of the larger philosophical picture.

Within legal systems, *insofar* as they exist and *so that* they can exist, attributions of validity are made. In fact, a legal system can only exist if the officials and institutions make these attributions jointly. This is facilitated by the rule of recognition, for its existence makes it possible for all involved to identify the same standards as applicable law. It only makes sense to engage in the language game of asserting claims concerning legal validity if others to whom the claims are addressed also carry out attributions of validity. If this condition is met, there is a rule of recognition. It would be misleading and wrong to regard this pragmatic condition for the success of moves in a language game as a 'hypothetical condition' of legal validity. Hart perceives this correctly. What Hart nevertheless overlooks is the transcendental function of common attributions. No legal knowledge – and no assertions – would be possible if the attributions of validity were not necessarily made jointly.[6]

## § 113

An idea as fundamental as the rule of recognition inevitably attracts controversy.

One such debate was triggered by Hart's late claim that the rule of recognition is a social convention.[7]

---

[6] For a pointed critical analysis, see SL Fish, 'Force' in his *Doing What Comes Naturally* (Oxford, Oxford University Press, 1989) 503–23.

[7] See Hart, n 2, 254–59. For an elaboration of a 'conventionalist' version of legal positivism, see Marmor, n 1, 36–83.

Conventions are arbitrary as to their substance, but permit achieving good goals if and as long as people adhere to them.

> *Initiate*: Driving on the left or right side of the street is an example of a convention; and so is the use of metal pieces and printed paper as carriers of exchange value.

On the condition that compliance with the convention in fact gives rise to a good result, it is morally obligatory to observe the convention.

> *Pupil*: As soon as the convention of driving on the left side of the street is de facto in force, it is my moral duty to act in accordance with it, for my compliance contributes to the prevention of accidents.

> *Realist*: You got it.

If the rule of recognition were indeed a convention, it would be morally obligatory for law-applying officials to respect it in order to sustain legal certainty. This moral duty, however, would be derivative of a requirement to strive for legal certainty. This norm, as we saw in our discussion of Radbruch's ideas (see § 78), is not absolute. Hence, the allegedly conventional quality of the rule of recognition does not constitute a sufficient ground of legal validity. The authority of the convention depends on moral grounds.

## § 114

The idea that legal certainty is to be achieved by following rules indicates what is the root of the failure and breakdown of modern legal positivism. Even in its late version, modern legal positivism focuses on norms as rules. The law consists of rules. This ontology is deeply questionable.

> *Reader*: Ontology?

> *Author*: Ontology is the teaching of what types of beings conceivably exist; or what something is, insofar as it is something and not nothing. 'Things' or 'facts' are the usual inventory of ontology.

## § 115

Rules of law can be seen either as a function of reasons for action or as detached from anything that may make action seem plausible.

In the first case, rules can be broken down into combinations of reasons. At bottom, they contain a reason for doing something in a certain situation.

What is decisive, however, for the quality of the rule is that another reason is added to the initial reason for action. The function of this further – second-order – reason is to ensure the relevance of the – first-order – reason for action in the situation envisaged by the rule. The second-order reason excludes balancing the relative weight of the first-order reason against other reasons. In this sense, Raz states that you are controlled by a rule when you have already decided in advance what to do in a certain situation.

> *Mother*: Please don't give me a fine. I'm in a hurry, my child has locked herself out of the apartment and I have to open the door.

> *Policewoman*: The law is the law. You have exceeded the speed limit.

This view of rules maintains their roots in morality. For whether and to what extent one is prepared to accept rules as unrelenting reasons for action is a moral question.

> *(The child sits in front of the apartment door and reads the first English translation of Kelsen's* Major Problems of Public Law Theory *with ostensible amusement)*

This understanding of rules has been developed by one of the most important legal positivists of our age, Joseph Raz.[8] Generally, however, legal positivists are inclined to endorse an understanding of rules that cuts the link to reasons for action. This stems from the fact that modern legal positivists are always keen on triangulating the normativity of law independently of morality. We have already encountered this ambition in the course of our discussion of Kelsen's primary legal norm.

A widespread strategy for conceiving of the bindingness of law while avoiding any connotations of morality is what can be called the 'semanticisation' of legal normativity.[9]

## § 116

Semantics is about the meaning of linguistic utterances and expressions.

Meaning can be understood as the properties of denotable objects (the 'intension' of the expression or the 'content of the concept').

> *Judge*: What do you mean by 'swine'?

> *Convict*: An animal with a corkscrew tail, ma'am.

---

[8] He developed his ideas concerning legal rules mostly in *Practical Reasons and Norms*, 3rd edn (Oxford, Oxford University Press, 1999).

[9] In my essay *Der Gegenstand der Rechtserkenntnis: Epitaph eines juristischen Problems* (Baden-Baden, Nomos, 1996) I offered a critique of semanticisation.

One also speaks of the 'meaning' of an expression, thereby designating the objects to which it applies.

> *Judge*: And who do you think is a 'Nazi'?
>
> *Convict*: Every member of the NSDAP.

Pragmatics is about the nuances of meaning that result from the use of language in specific contexts and about the actions that are carried out through the use of language, the so-called 'speech acts' (such as assertions, questions, apologies, etc.).

> *Judge*: So, in the previous chapter you wanted to say that I am an animal with a corkscrew tail belonging to the NSDAP?'
>
> *Convict*: Oh no, that was just an attempt to hide my love.
>
> *Judge*: So you didn't mean to insult me?
>
> *Convict*: What are you thinking, your Honour!
>
> *Judge (opens her handbag and takes out a cigarette, lights it up and watches the rising smoke; with a mild and yet ailing look at the convict)*: You're my boy, aren't you?

Both semantics and pragmatics can be applied quite rigidly. Speech act theory is inclined to do that. The conventional rules of language are taken to be decisive for the meaning of expressions and speech acts,[10] regardless of what the intention of the speaker might be.

Underlying this rigidity, as Jacques Derrida perceptively observed, is a propensity to 'juridify' language.[11] Remarkably, it is a projection onto language of the solidity that legal positivists would like the law to possess by virtue of language.

In general, legal scholars have a terrible tendency to expect language to behave like a mechanical system. They are inclined to view it as a conventional system of rules that convey a certain meaning automatically.

But first things first.

---

[10] Speech-act theory has been developed in two classic works: JL Austin, *How to Do Things With Words* (Cambridge, MA, Harvard University Press, 1962) and JR Searle, *Speech Acts: An Essay in the Philosophy of Language* (London, Cambridge University Press, 1969).

[11] See J Derrida, *Limited Inc* (trans S Weber, Evanston, IL, Northwestern University Press, 1988) 76, 91, 132.

§ 117

One encounters semanticisation in the context of legal interpretation. It is manifest in the substitution of any morally significant discussion of the issues with an analysis of the meaning of linguistic expressions.

Linguistic rules determine correct language use. They are normative.

> ~~*Thinker*~~: He who calls a canary a 'sow' commits a mistake.

> *Author*: Will you shut up!

With the aid of semanticisation, the normativity of law can draw on the bindingness of language rules.

> *Pupil*: Language! Ah …

A rule of law must be applied to the facts which are specified in the antecedent condition of the norm. The rules for the correct use of the concepts relevant to the description of an offence are language rules.

> *Judge*: The ban on keeping domestic sows in residential neighbourhoods also applies to canaries.

> *Initiate (beside himself and gesticulating wildly)*: A sow is a sow and not a canary. I will not put up with this nonsense!

Modern legal positivism, once it is in demise, finally discovers in language the morally independent normativity which it has always sought. As a system of rules, the law can exercise its guiding and critical function if one adheres to the language rules governing the use of the terms to be found in legal rules. The bindingness of language rules is independent of morality.

> *Pupil, child, judge, mother and reader (rhythmically in a chorus line, arms raised, fingers snapping and rocking)*: A sow is a sow is a sow. A sow is a sow is a sow.

Why isn't this the happy ending?

§ 118

> *Author and poet at a pond. The poet lies in the grass, his legs up, and smokes a joint. The author jumps up.*

> *Author (to the poet)*: Think of an example.

*Poet*: But thinking is darn hard.

*Author*: C'mon.

## § 119

*Poet*: A local police ordinance says: 'No dogs in the park'.

*Author*: Why, thank you!

The bindingness of a local police decree prohibiting the bringing of dogs into a park is manifested in the fact that the language rules for the term 'dog' control the application of the norm.

*Mother*: No guide dogs either? This would exclude disabled people from a public space.

*Supernanny*: This is an outrage!

*Newman*: A dog is a dog is a dog.

*The pupil, child, judge, mother and reader are all of a sudden torn from their ecstasy and stare into the distance with an empty gaze.*

The mere relevance of the question whether the local police ordinance is also applicable to guide dogs proves that the moral understanding of rules is never completely suspended. Evidently, a guide dog is also a 'dog'. Nevertheless, something makes us reluctant to include such an animal into the scope of application of this rule. That is why, at this juncture, either the semanticisation of legal rules is dropped again in favour of purposive interpretations; or, alternatively, the question raised by our moral sentiments is answered with recourse to a source, for example by asking what the issuing authorities had in mind when they adopted the ordinance. The corresponding historical research does not amount to a mere application of language rules and is afflicted with various difficulties. In any case, it reintroduces into legal positivism the conception of the legal norm as a command, which is difficult to reconcile with the prior emphasis on a conventional understanding of language.

In both cases, the semanticisation of the obligation turns out to be a hopeless path. It even looks like a diversionary tactic.

## § 120

The semanticisation of the bindingness of law is based on the idea that the legal rule – the norm – controls its own application. When a dog comes by, the prohibition snaps shut like a trap.

> *The poet sits by the pond with his legs outstretched and smiles foolishly, while a dog howls in the background.*

But this idea is abstract. First, the meaning of terms can only be sharpened in light of situations. It is through concrete encounters that we discover what we 'really' mean by a term.

> *Pupil (sitting on a park bench stroking the guide dog)*: No, you are not an ordinary dog, you are something very special.

> *Poet (as if in trance)*: The abundance of the word entices language to speak.

Secondly, a legal rule cannot itself check whether it is relevant to the case. It presupposes the interpreter's prior understanding of the situation.

## § 121

The first to confront modern legal positivism with these hermeneutic insights was Kelsen's disciple Fritz Sander.[12]

It was mentioned above that for Kelsen the transfer of validity takes place within a hierarchical structure. The application of the higher-ranking norms confers validity on the lower-ranking norms, at least so long as the application observes the framework established by the higher norm.

> *Law*: Anyone who takes a movable object away from another with the intention of unlawfully enriching himself or a third party

---

[12] Some of Sander's writings are collected in SL Paulson (ed), *Die Rolle des Neukantianismus in der Reinen Rechtslehre: Eine Debatte zwischen Sander und Kelsen* (Aalen, Scientia, 1988). A reinvigoration of Sander's ideas can be found in C Kletzer, 'Absolute Positivism' (2013) 42 *Netherlands Journal of Legal Philosophy* 87–99. Adolf Julius Merkl's criticism of Sander is documented in his *Die Lehre von der Rechtskraft entwickelt aus dem Rechtsbegriff: Eine rechtstheoretische Untersuchung* (Leipzig, Deuticke, 1923). For a historical perspective, see AJ Korb, *Kelsens Kritiker: Ein Beitrag zur Geschichte der Rechts- und Staatstheorie (1911–1934)* (Tübingen, Mohr, 2010).

by appropriating the object is to be punished with a custodial sentence of up to six months.

*Judge*: I hereby sentence you to three months in prison for theft.

*Convict (to judge)*: You Nazi swine!

Within the hierarchical structure of law creation, the transfer-of-validity relationship runs linearly from the top to the bottom. It is as though the higher norm said to the lower:

*Higher norm (solemnly)*:   Yes, you descend from me, you are my progeny.

Sander appears to have understood that this idea does not accurately reflect the *social* validity on which legal validity is based (see § 104). After all, anyone who imposes fines or executes the dirty work of foreclosure at a lower (and lowlier) level of law creation has to make sure that he or she is covered by one or the other legal norm. Those norms come into perspective against the backdrop of pragmatic exigences. Their meaning is thereby affected.

*Bombarded civilian*: Why do you go after my life?

*UN Security Council*: Your government is about to commit genocide and this behaviour represents a 'threat to world peace'. That's why we've taken action against your country. We are sorry.

*Child (to judge)*: I don't like your dress.

*Judge*: The right to respect my private life permits me to appear in public as I wish, at least as long as I do not violate standards of public decency.

*Constitutional Court*: The principle of equality enshrines a general principle of reasonableness that applies even without any comparison between or among situations or groups.

Norms become effective only because there are people on the ground who take them to mean certain things. They draw on these understanding in order to justify or rationalise their behaviour. The attribution of meaning begins, so to speak, from below. In Sander's words, this means that the condition of the creation of a norm serves as such a condition only *for* – and from the perspective of – the created norm. Sander states this as follows:

Not only B as legal consequence is determined by A as legal condition, but also in the opposite direction A as legal condition determines itself in view of B as legal consequence. A and B determine each other mutually ....[13]

It is essential that the determination is mutual. A reversal of the hierarchy alone would again result in a hierarchy, even if it were a hierarchy turned upside down.

Remarkably, while the elementary relation of the hierarchy envisaged by legal positivists is blind obedience, the basic relation of social validity is rationalisation.

> *Hierarchy*: A sow is a sow is a sow.
>
> *The pupil, child, judge, mother and reader are briefly thrown into raptures again.*
>
> *Reverse hierarchy*: I get to decide who's a sow.

The idea of the hierarchical structure is too naïve to grasp how the transfer of validity really works. Allowing outright reversals of the hierarchy to go forward would, by contrast, be too frivolous. It would open the gate to arbitrary decisions. This may be the reason why Sander talks about a mutual determination. It can be fathomed as an infinite mutual mirroring. This means that the applicable legal norm determines the applicable act in the same way as the applicable act determines the applicable norm. Both, in a sense, permit this. They consider it appropriate and correct.

> *Norm (to the judgement)*: You're my judgement, for you have understood what I want.
>
> *Judgement (to the norm)*: You're my norm, because you fit my case perfectly well.

## § 122

What can guarantee that the norm and the judgement are not talking past one another? Here is Sander's answer: 'A and B determined each other mutually, rather, they are determined mutually with a process that is carried out according to higher order laws'.[14] It is the 'sovereign' legal procedure

---

[13] See F Sander, 'Die transzendentale Methode der Rechtsphilosophie und der Begriff der Rechtserfahrung' (1920) in Paulson (ed), n 12, 75–114, 102–03 (my translation).
[14] ibid 103 (my translation).

pursuant to (unknown) 'higher-order laws' that establishes agreement between the two.

The term 'procedure' stands here for the real dynamic of the entire legal system. It is this encompassing totality that guarantees the handshake between the norm ('You are my judgement') and the judgement ('You are my norm').

Sander emphasises the synthetic quality of legal knowledge. In a strong analogy to Kant's idea that in a judgment sensual intuition and the concept-forming understanding work together in order to provide us with new experience,[15] Sander emphasises the connection established between 'sensations of justice' and legal norms. What may intuitively appear right to us is amenable to objective validation by finding the appropriate legal condition. Whether this happens or not is a historical question. The totality that guarantees the complementarity of the perspectives 'from above' and 'from below' must be taken for granted. Sander advances therewith, without being aware of it, to a conception of law *qua* objective spirit.

## § 123

The expression 'objective spirit' does not designate anything highfalutin. It is about something simple that is merely eclipsed by the presence of too much false legal theory. Law is not a set of norms. It is a human practice. It is a practice of judgment based on knowing what the law is. This knowledge is shared among legal officials.[16]

In his confrontation with Adolf Julius Merkl, Sander takes the side of the objective, institutionally manifest spirit and rejects the subjective spirit of the individual legal scholars as irrelevant. Only legal knowledge that succeeds at asserting itself within the legal system communicates law. In this vein, Kelsen attributed to Sander the following view: 'There is no real legal science, as I claim, but only law, but the law itself is – a science'.[17] We shall come back to this (see § 129).

---

[15] See I Kant, *Critique of Pure Reason* (trans P Guyer and A Wood, Cambridge, Cambridge University Press, 1998) B 93, p 205.

[16] For a more elaborate conception of objective spirit, see RB Pippin, *Hegel's Practical Philosophy: Rational Agency as Ethical Life* (Cambridge, Cambridge University Press, 2008) 242. See also T Pinkard, *Hegel's Phenomenology: The Sociality of Reason* (Cambridge, Cambridge University Press, 1994) 122–24.

[17] H Kelsen, 'Rechtswissenschaft und Recht: Erledigung eines Versuchs zur Überwindung der "Rechtsdogmatik"' (1922) in Paulson (ed), n 12, 279–411, 377 (my translation).

## § 124

Sander thus anticipated the legal theory that Niklas Luhmann would develop 60 to 70 years later. By adopting an objectifying (rather than performative) attitude towards the sovereign process of law creation, Sander provides a sociological account of the interwovenness of law and legal knowledge. In many respects it resembles Luhmann's later sociological theory of law:

> *Reader*: What is a 'performative attitude'?
>
> *Author*: A performative attitude is adopted by those who take claims to validity seriously and actively engage with them. For example, one approaches the law with this attitude when one discusses the rationality of certain rules. If one merely takes cognisance of the existence of rules, the attitude is objectifying.
>
> *Child*: The term was coined by Jürgen Habermas.[18]
>
> *Author*: Habermas! Ah …

According to Luhmann, the legal system is composed of communications.[19] These are guided by one fundamental distinction, which is – surprise! – the distinction between legal and illegal. Any communication that uses this distinction (Luhmann calls it the 'code') explicitly or implicitly is part of the legal system. The only question is whether and how far a communication can create resonance.

> *Poet*: It is an illegality that I am poor.
>
> *Mother*: You have no reason to complain.

Luhmann counts among the 'operations' of the legal system those communications claiming that something is legal or illegal. Operations place themselves within the system by drawing on previously determined law. Just like Sander before him, Luhmann perceives no asymmetry in the relation between before and after. It is not the case, that is, that either is subordinate

---

[18] See, for example, J Habermas, *Diskursethik*, Philosophische Texte vol 3, 4th edn (Berlin, Suhrkamp, 2019) 424.
[19] Niklas Luhmann's work on legal theory is also very extensive. Three works, however, have what it takes to become classics: his early *A Sociological Theory of Law* (trans E King and M Albrow, London, Routledge and Kegan Paul, 1985); *Law as a Social System* (trans A Ziegert, Oxford, Oxford University Press, 2004); and *Legitimation durch Verfahren*, 4th edn (Frankfurt aM, Suhrkamp, 1986), the latter having made him famous right away.

to the other. Hence, Luhmann speaks of 'recursive symmetry' and articulates Sander's insight most clearly:

> The norm quality of each element is due to the norm quality of other elements, of which the same is true. Therefore, there can be no hierarchy of norms. Even between laws and judicial decisions there is, as regards normativity, a strictly symmetrical relationship. Laws are taken to be norms only because they are intended to be applied in decisions, just as these decisions can regulate situations only because this is provided for in laws. As far as normativity is concerned, there is, hence, a circular relation between rule and the rule-applying decision.[20]

Luhmann's legal system consists of the concatenation of partial perspectives on the law that flare up, as it were, in individual decisions; but they can never add up to a coherent whole. The pleasantly hierarchically structured images of law that we encounter in textbooks are simplifications in which the complexity of actual events is reduced for the purpose of guiding behaviour. The legal knowledge that is fed into the reproduction of the legal system is much simpler than the system itself.

## § 125

According to Luhmann, modern law is also a recursively closed system. This means that new law can only be created out of other law, and not out of morality or economic rationality. The law that is relied upon in order to create more law is itself a product of the system. That is why Luhmann considers the law to be an 'autopoietic' system. It generates itself from itself. The element to be created selects the elements from which it is to be created. The system is therefore inevitably circular.

> *Child*: But must not there be a first law, an arch-law, as it were?

> *Pupil*: No, I believe there is always only a circle. A piece of legislation is a norm for the reason that a court judgment bases itself on it. The judgment can be a norm for the reason that there is a piece of legislation backing it up. The judgment is a norm for the reason of being based on a piece of legislation that is relevant for backing up judgments.

---

[20] N Luhmann, 'Die Einheit des Rechtssystems' (1983) 14 *Rechtstheorie* 129–54, 140 (my translation).

*Child*: But why this detour? Why doesn't the judgment immediately say what it actually does, namely that it establishes itself as a law? Why doesn't Luhmann embrace Frank's decision theory of law?

*Pupil*: I don't know.

*(The initiate has returned to his office and pulls off the shelves one volume after the other of a 12-volume encyclopaedia on Luhmann's work, nervously searching for something.)*

What is more, the inevitable circular system must presuppose itself in order to bring itself into being and to preserve itself. In this context, Luhmann speaks of the 'self-implification' of the system. In order to select the elements from which it is to be created, the legal system must posit itself into existence.

*Child*: This is even more ambitious than the ontological proof of God!

*Author*: Definitely, it reminds me of the German idealist philosophy conceived of the thinking subject, the 'I', as positing itself into existence in the act of thinking.[21]

*Reader*: I don't want to hear this!

## § 126

The self-presupposition of the system is elementary and implicit.

Each operation of the system involves two observations. One says that something has happened, and the other that the observed event is legal or illegal. Since the latter observation observes the former, the systems consist of 'second-order observations' or, as Luhmann also puts it, of 'observations of observations'.

*Child (to the poet)*: You are poor.

*Poet (to the audience)*: That's a grave injustice!

Such observations reveal the difference between the system and the environment. The external reference to what is observed as legal or illegal refers

---

[21] A crisp introduction to the idea of the self-positing I, as it appears in Fichte's transcendental philosophy, is offered by E Förster, *The Twenty-Five Years of Philosophy: A Systematic Reconstruction* (trans B Bowman, Cambridge, MA, Harvard University Press, 2012) 179–82.

to the system's environment, the system's reference to itself is implied in the reference to one or the other of its elements.

> *Reader.* But that's a lot of terminology for not so riveting thoughts.

> *Author.* I know! Over four decades Luhmann repeatedly recon- ceived and rebuilt his theory by importing different basic concepts from other disciplines, such as biology or cybernetics. Initially, the distinction between the system and its environment was of key importance, which was then superseded with self-reference and autopoiesis until he, finally, concluded with 'second-order cybernetics', ie the observation of observations. If you write about Luhmann, you have to take all periods into account. That's pretty exasperating.

> *Reader.* Don't expect me to feel sorry for you. You have chosen to come up with this fudge.

As soon as the identity of the system becomes an issue for itself, the distinc- tion between the law and that which is different from it enters the legal system itself. The law then produces an account of what sets it apart from other phenomena.

What lends unity to the legal system – the equivalent of Sander's totality, which we have called the 'objective spirit' – are once again only differences. What is the law? It is not what is happening in its environment, and it is not art, religion, the economy, education and so forth. The unity of the system exists only as difference, and the difference never transcends the negativity of bad infinity.

> *Reader.* O boy, where is that coming from?

> *Author.* Infinity is bad if you can move forward indefinitely and never stop anywhere because a sequence is going on forever. The law is always cast as 'different from' something else. Its essence is to be 'not something else'. Infinity is good when something is not limited from the outside, but by itself – by its concept, that is.

> *Reader.* You have taken this out of Hegel, haven't you?

> *Author.* If you say so.[22]

---

[22] See, for example, S Houlgate, *The Opening of Hegel's Logic: From Being to Infinity* (West Lafayette, Purdue University Press, 2006) 312–30.

§ 127

Like any other system, the legal system is circular. That explains why it is, according to Luhmann, a wellspring of 'paradoxes', the simplest of which says that all law is injustice: *summum ius, summa iniuria.*

> *Pupil*: I think I got it. The judgment says about itself that it is legal by presupposing a law that empowers it to administer justice. In response to such a judgment a convict can claim that this presupposition is illegal because it is legally unfounded.
>
> *Convict (offstage)*: You Nazi swine!
>
> *Child*: How does that help me to understand?
>
> *Pupil*: Look, we discover one operation in the system that assigns the code value 'legal' to a certain event and another operation that reverses the assignment to 'illegal'. It is like turning a switch from 'on' to 'off'. If we abstract from the fact that the court has higher authority than the convicted person, we get a situation in which the system says 'The conviction of the convicted person is right and wrong' or 'The convicted person has been unlawfully and lawfully convicted'.
>
> *Child*: And how does *that* help me to understand?

§ 128

Operations of the legal system constitute the authority on which they make themselves dependent. At the same time, they would have to be empowered by this authority to undergird this dependence. Kelsen reached no different conclusion when he characterised the basic norm as a fiction (see § 105). Moreover, the law operates self-referentially. As a result, the code of legal and illegal can be applied to thus coded communications at any time. Hence, the following possibility can never be excluded:

> *Poet*: It is illegal that this is law.

If something is legal and illegal at the same time, the legal system obviously no longer produces any legal knowledge. Without such knowledge, however, there can be no law. The system is blocked.

> *The pupil, child, judge, mother and reader stand there with their mouths open and stare into the void.*

Blockages in the legal system can only be overcome by ditching the tie between legality and illegality.

The tie arises owing to the initial indeterminacy of the coding. In its hypothetical initial state it does not matter which code value is assigned to events. The system is therefore only stuck with a 'paradox' as long as it lacks the so-called programs.

Programs regulate the assignment of code values. They can be either conditional ('if, then') or final ('realise x') and are used in order to eradicate paradoxes from the system. They accomplish this by permitting the code to enter into that which has already been distinguished by the code (eg by stating 'This has been illegally coded as legal'). As soon as there are programs – rules – it is possible to distinguish between lawful and unlawful allocations of code values. This does not mean that the creation of programs, which then coalesce into the 'structures' of the system, prevents the occurrence of paradoxes. But what can be accomplished is to marginalise and thus to 'invisibilise' their occurrence.

On the level of programs, the unity of the system – ie the code with its two sides – makes its appearance within the system as the programs determine the correct allocation of the code values. On the inside of this unity there is 'law' and on the 'outside' there is everything that is illegal.

Differentiation is, however, the hallmark of the legal system as a whole. In this respect, *as* a two-sided distinction it also possesses another outer side. It cannot observe it. Only external observers can explain to the legal system what it does not perceive when it assigns the code values.

| inside | | outside |
|---|---|---|
| inside: 'legal' | outside: 'illegal' | non-law |

*Author (smirking)*: Enough?

*Reader (startled out of his sleep)*: The code, the basic norm, they have all turned against me!

## § 129

Both Kelsen and his disciple Merkl objected to Sander's theory. He leaves no room, they said, for that legal scholarship which does not feed into the operations of the legal system. Knowledge of the law has its place only in the context of the sovereign procedure of law production.

Merkl perceived clearly that legal knowledge could in principle be manifest within two different legal systems, namely in one that consists of the de facto concatenation of enforceable decisions, and in another that is the offshoot of legal science, however without actual power of decision making. Merkl considered the discovery of true law to be the province of scholarship, a view he defended with much pathos and not with characteristic legal positivist sobriety. Only legal science can give us the true law.

In a manner strongly reminiscent of Sander, Luhmann views the legal system sustained through recursive operations that produce law owing to the connection that they establish with prior decisions. They thus both implicitly accede to the view of the legal realists that only a decision which is presumably relevant for future cases introduces something like a legal norm. Ultimately, however, all concatenations are 'fatal' in the sense that they just happen, no matter what the odds are for or against their occurrence.[23]

Once positivism is overcome, we fall back on legal realism.

This is not necessarily a bad thing.

§ 130

Late legal positivism does not fare any better. It relies on a conventionalist view of language. According to this view, concepts establish arbitrary linkages between signs and classes of objects. The meaning is shaped by their use. The use is manifest in linguistic conventions.

The term 'bathroom' is utilised in American English for something different than in British English. One masters the meaning of a term by using it as every competent speaker does.

> *Initiate*: With which word do folks in North America refer to the
> toilet?

---

[23] I would like to draw the attention of readers to the fact that Gunther Teubner is another important legal systems theorist. He has worked much on problems of legal control failure and globalisation. His main work in legal theory and his most recent contribution to constitutional theory are just two examples: *Law as an Autopoietic System* (Oxford, Basil Blackwell, 1989); *Constitutional Fragments* (Oxford, Oxford University Press, 2012). Another important representative of this approach is Karl-Heinz Ladeur. See his *Postmoderne Rechtstheorie: Selbstreferenz – Selbstorganisation – Prozeduralisierung* (Berlin, Duncker & Humblot, 1995) and *Die Textualität des Rechts. Zur poststrukturalistischen Kritik des Rechts* (Weilerswist, Velbrück Verlag, 2005); I Augsberg, *Die Lesbarkeit des Rechts. Texttheoretische Lektionen für eine postmoderne juristische Methodologie* (Weilerswist, Velbrück, 2009). See also T Gostomzyk and L Viellechner (eds), *Denken in Netzwerken: Zur Rechts- und Gesellschaftstheorie von Karl-Heinz Ladeur* (Tübingen, Mohr, 2009).

> *Pupil*: 'Bathroom'.
>
> *Initiate*: And what do they call our 'bathroom'?
>
> *Pupil*: 'Bath'.

Once one has acquired a certain confidence in the use of linguistic conventions, one can try one's hand at explicating its meaning by using the first-person plural.

> *Pupil*: In America we call the room that includes a bath, a shower, a washbasin, and possibly even a toilet the 'bath'.
>
> *Child*: But you're not American.

Pragmatically, one absorbs conventions on the basis of doing two things. On the one hand, one immerses oneself in the practice through cautiously trying to do as all others do and, on the other, one engages in courageous attempts to assert one's own understanding of the practice as the practice itself.

But linguistic rules are not mere empirical regularities.[24]

> *Pupil (with 3D glasses on, placed in front of a screen, onto which different photos of pigs are projected, one after the other)*: Sow. Sow. Sow. Sow. Sow.

According to a late positivist view, linguistic rules are manifest in social practices, but this does not mean that they are mere regularities. The possibility of 'making mistakes' is part of the existence of the 'rule', as Wittgenstein memorably noted.[25]

> *Pupil*: Wittgenstein! Ah.
>
> *Initiate*: Did you even realise that your answer was wrong? There were only four sows.

---

[24] For a rejection of 'regularism' see, again, RB Brandom, *Making it Explicit: Reasoning, Representing, and Discursive Commitment* (Cambridge, MA, Harvard University Press, 1994) 27–28, and § 77.

[25] See L Wittgenstein, *Philosophical Investigations*, 3rd edn (trans GEM Anscombe, Oxford, Blackwell, 2001) § 202. Wittgenstein's views on rules are subject to various elaborations. I am merely mentioning SR Kripke, *Wittgenstein on Rules and Private Language: An Elementary Exposition* (Cambridge, MA, Harvard University Press, 1982); for an account of its effects and the rebuttals that Kripke's work has given rise to, see S Hershovitz, 'Wittgenstein on Rules: The Phantom Menace' (2002) 22 *Oxford Journal of Legal Studies* 619–40. Wittgenstein-based approaches to legal theory are offered by A Marmor, *Interpretation and Legal Theory* (Oxford, Clarendon Press, 1992), B Bix, *Law, Language and Legal Determinacy* (Oxford, Clarendon Press, 1993), D Patterson, *Law and Truth* (New York, Oxford University Press, 1996). See also F Müller and R Christensen, *Juristische Methodik, Grundlegung für die Arbeitsmethoden der Rechtspraxis*, vol 1, 11th edn (Berlin, Duncker & Humblot, 2013).

According to Hart, the normative dimension of rules is manifest in the critical attitude with which one observes one's own behaviour and that of others. But if the criterion on which this attitude draws for the purpose of critique cannot coincide with the actual behaviour because the correct and incorrect use of language could not be distinguished in this way, it is necessary to develop an idea – a 'conception' – of the meaning of the rule. There has to be an understanding of the rule that goes beyond the aggregation of individual applications. Such an understanding must show why it makes sense to regard a thing as a 'bathroom'. It has to provide us with clues. These are brought into play in normative accounts of the use of words.

> *Judge*: Of course, this is a 'bathroom', it has a stool.

There is no meaning without a possible explication. By developing an understanding of what lends it authority and by regenerating itself with having recourse to an account of itself, a linguistic practice appears in the gestalt of 'spirit'.

Positivism has never arrived at this insight.

## § 131

Fortifying the bindingness of law by semantic means is a substitute construction. It loses its spell as soon as one examines more closely how the determination of meanings really works.

Above all, the semanticised ideals of bindingness are always susceptible to being shattered from a moral perspective.

> *Mother*: Guide dogs must be admitted to the park. Otherwise, the dog ban would amount to a ban on blind persons.
>
> *Initiate*: A dog is a dog is a dog. If we gave up the commitment to the wording, the law could not exercise any social control, and nobody would know what to expect.

The commitment to semantics thus turns out to be morally grounded. Possibly, the former is only a facade on the part of legal positivists to hide their morally affirmative relationship to legality. They want to believe in the power of semantic normativity because of the great moral value that they attach to legal certainty.

Moreover, legal positivists generally turn their backs on how we go about calibrating the relevance and scope of application of semantic rules. Once we look more closely, it turns out that the law is not just rules.

> *Mother:* A ban on dogs that extended also to guide dogs would exclude and discriminate against particularly vulnerable people. Making an exception for guide dogs would not affect legal certainty too much because there are rarely any other cases imaginable in which patrons of a public park depend on a dog's assistance.

The arguments concerning the relevance of rules do not themselves draw on rules. Rather, they resort to principles. The inclusion of people in public spaces is one such principle and legal certainty is another.

If a rule is interpreted contrary to its wording in order to make room for a principle, the importance of realising this principle must be weighed against legal certainty. From this it can be seen that in contrast to rules that apply in an 'all or nothing' fashion, principles possess the dimension of weight. They incline the resolution of a case in a certain direction without necessitating the result.

Ronald Dworkin's legal theory, which he presented as a radical critique of late legal positivism, began with this observation.[26] He immediately went on to explain that principles are often not positive law, but originate from the broader moral background of law. Thus, with the demise of the semanticisation of legal validity the strict separation of law and morality becomes rejected as well.

---

[26] See R Dworkin, 'The Model of Rules I' in his *Taking Rights Seriously*, 2nd edn (Cambridge, MA, Harvard University Press, 1978) 22–45.

# Objective Spirit

## § 132

There is another criticism of modern legal positivism. It is not an internal critique that takes premises for granted in order to argue that a position does not live up to them. But it is no less powerful. The objection made to legal positivism is, rather, that it misrepresents how legal knowledge really works. More precisely, the criticism claims that legal positivism's attempt to preserve the relevance of normativity that is inherent in the practice of knowing the law fails for the reason that it does not adequately capture what this normativity really is.

All right, this may even amount to an internal critique.

Those raising and defending legal knowledge claims consider the law to be binding. At least they purport to obtain guidance from it. Legal positivism reconstructs this attitude in such a manner that those raising and defending legal claims are taken to conceive of the law invariably as a system of rules. But this involves a misunderstanding. The social validity of law – its efficacy as a normative standard (see § 104) – is not only, let alone exclusively, manifest in adherence to rules.

## § 133

One discovers this critical perspective originally in the work of Carl Schmitt. He presents it in a short tract published in 1934. The text was supposed to blaze the trail for legal renewal in Nazi Germany. It is entitled *The Three Types of Legal Thought* and should be studied with much caution.[1]

> *Convict (offstage)*: You Nazi swine!

> *Judge (also offstage)*: Shut up!

---

[1] Carl Schmitt's *Über die drei Arten des Rechtswissenschaftlichen Denkens* (Hamburg, Hanseatische Verlagsanstalt, 1934) is to be seen in the context of National Socialist legal theory. This is now comprehensively documented in the anthology J Pauer-Studer and J Fink (eds), *Rechtfertigungen des Unrechts: Das Rechtsdenken des Nationalsozialismus in Originaltexten* (Berlin, Suhrkamp, 2014). There is an English translation of Schmitt's pamphlet, but it shows that it was prepared by a legal scholar. C Schmitt, *On the Three Types of Juristic Thought* (trans J Bendersky, Westport, CT, Praeger, 2004).

Carl Schmitt was neither a follower nor a hack. He was a forerunner and, indeed, a leader. After the Nazis' seizure of power, he immediately made himself available to the party as a legal apologist and became a spokesperson for the 'renewal' of the administration of justice in Germany. That he had a falling-out with the party in the early 1940s is a different matter.

Intellectuals who, like Schmitt, Martin Heidegger or Anton von Webern, were fascinated with National Socialism or at least saw in it a vehicle for their own advancement, did not suffer from a sudden loss of intelligence. Schmitt's tract is sharp. Although his text performs a deep bow to the movement and its rulers and also contains appalling anti-Semitic allusions, it is nonetheless a remarkable contribution to legal theory. Schmitt's approach has precursors in Maurice Hauriou or Santi Romano and knows later representatives like Peter Häberle, Neil MacCormick and Ota Weinberger.[2] Schmitt's text is, however, unsurpassed in its originality and ingenuity.

> *Convict (to the author)*: You Nazi swine!

## § 134

> *A squat little man enters the stage. In passing, he takes an indignant look at the convict. He steps to the lectern and begins to declaim with a strongly rolling R*: Every lawyer who, consciously or unconsciously, bases his work on a concept of '*law*' grasps the law either as a *rule*, or as a *decision*, or as a *concrete order and formation* (Gestaltung). Therefore, three types of legal thinking can be determined. They are distinguished here.[3]

---

[2] For a most comprehensive introduction to 'institutionalism', see M La Torre, *Law as Institution* (Dordrecht, Springer, 2010). B Rüthers, *Institutionelles Rechtsdenken im Wandel der Verfassungsepochen* (Berlin, Gehlen, 1970). On the French origins, see A Broderick (ed), *The French Institutionalists: Maurice Hauriou, Georges Renard, Joseph T. Delos* (trans M Welling, Cambridge, MA, Harvard University Press, 1970); M Hauriou, *Tradition in Social Science* (trans CB Gray, Amsterdam, Rodopi, 2011); CB Gray, *The Methodology of Maurice Hauriou: Legal, Sociological, Philosophical* (Amsterdam, Rodopi, 2010). For the Italian variety, see S Romano, *The Legal Order* (trans M Croce, Abingdon, Routledge, 2017). On Schmitt's reception, see M De Wilde, 'The Dark Side of Constitutionalism: Carl Schmitt Reading Santi Romano' (2018) 11 *Ethics & Global Politics* 12–24. A fine example of the productive application of Hauriou's ideas is Peter Häberle's *Die Wesensgehaltsgarantie des Art. 19 Abs. 2 des Grundgesetzes*, 3rd edn (Heidelberg, C.F. Müller, 1983). Institutional legal thinking had a brief renaissance with the publication of N MacCormick and O Weinberger, *An Institutional Theory of Law* (Dordrecht, Reidel, 1986).

[3] Schmitt, *Über die drei Arten*, n 1, 7 (my translation).

## § 135

As so often in the case of Schmitt, the text is a pamphlet. Legal positivism is the chosen opponent.

What confers distinction on Schmitt as a critic, generally, is his ability to expose as composites of heterogeneous parts those positions that present themselves as coherent wholes. Instead of being one they turn out to have been pasted together from two or even three.

> *Mother (to the crying child)*: Why are you doing this? I don't even know you like that. That's not you.

Schmitt's strategy is developed particularly clearly in his constitutional theory.[4] There, the liberal democratic constitutional state is made to understand that it is a hodgepodge of two heterogeneous elements: a legal and a political one. The modern democratic constitutional state is thus exposed as a mixed constitution, more precisely, as a mixture of aristocratic and democratic elements. In his criticism of the Weimar Constitution,[5] Schmitt points out that it is again made up of two or three competing conceptions of political authority. The constitution of the parliamentary 'legislative state' is supplemented by the constitution pursuant to which measures are taken in response to pressing exigencies. Finally, the fundamental right section represents even a 'counter-constitution'.

Schmitt uses this strategy in order to make us see separation instead of unity. The relevant divisions do not only possess political salience. They confront us with an intellectual predicament. If one is confronted with genuine separateness, then there is nothing that can possibly mediate between and among heterogeneous elements. Any arrangement reached must remain a contingent and brittle *modus vivendi*, which can be neither fully justified nor understood. The relation between the divided elements is not amenable to a rational justification going beyond the admission that some accommodation had to be found in order to prevent strife.

> *Judge (to the convict)*: I never know where I am with you. You're always either like this or like that.

We shall return to the subject of division in the next chapter.

---

[4] There is a translation of Schmitt's *Verfassungslehre* available as *Constitutional Theory* (trans J Seitzer, Durham, NC, Duke University Press, 2008).

[5] The vivisection of the Weimar Constitution is carried out in *Legality and Legitimacy* (trans J Seitzer, Durham, NC, Duke University Press, 2004).

## § 136

Legal positivism presents itself as a coherent account of legal theory. According to Schmitt, it is, however, internally split. It is a composite of two positions. Schmitt calls one 'normativism' and the other 'decisionism'.[6] In the eyes of legal positivists, the law consists of rules. This is a manifestation of normativism. Should the rules run out, the law is to be determined on the basis of a discretionary decision (see Kelsen's basic operation § 93). This is indicative of decisionism. Legally speaking, within the scope left open for discretion only a pure decision is possible. What happens then amounts to a creation from nothing, a *creatio ex nihilo*.

> *Judge*: The law provides for a punishment of five to ten years of imprisonment. I'll make you serve nine-and-a-half.
>
> *The convict is gagged and tied to a chair. His entire head is wrapped in a bandage. As if he were trying to free himself, he slides wildly back and forth and throws his upper body forward. He tries to yell something, but his voice is suffocated by the gag.*
>
> *Poet*: This decision is a miracle.

Before we look at Schmitt's understanding of these two positions, let us briefly anticipate Ronald Dworkin. In their characterisation of legal positivism, Schmitt and Dworkin could not agree more. Dworkin says about positivism that it understands the law as a system of rules. These rules are applicable in an 'all or nothing' fashion. But as soon as the rules run out the baton is handed over to discretion. Discretion is externally limited, but internally unlimited. It is like a 'hole in a doughnut', namely a normative nil surrounded by a belt of restrictions. Within this belt the decision makers enjoy complete freedom. The decision is miraculously born out of a limited normative void.[7]

## § 137

And yet, Schmitt's characterisation of legal positivism as a heterogeneous combination of normativism and decisionism is more nuanced than

---

[6] See Schmitt, *Three Types*, n 1, 67.
[7] See R Dworkin, 'The Model of Rules I' in his *Taking Rights Seriously*, 2nd edn (Cambridge, MA, Harvard University Press, 1978) 22–45, 26, 31.

Dworkin's view of legal positivism as a set of ideas about law as a system of rules. What legal positivism stands for is actually more adequately captured by Schmitt.

Schmitt says that from the perspective of normativists the law is composed of general rules. These rules apply without paying attention to the status of the person affected. Generality guarantees impartiality and impersonality. It facilitates 'a government of laws, and not of men' (as John Adams famously put it). Adjudicating matters means to apply these laws *sine ira et studio*.

> *Judge*: As a human being I am entirely dispensable. I am an automaton subsuming descriptions of facts under general legal rules.

> *The convict shouts something – albeit incomprehensible – into the gag.*

In the universe of normativism, there is no place for a personal relationship between the rulers and the ruled. There is only the norm, on the one side, and conforming or deviating behaviour, on the other. A personal relationship of loyalty between leaders and followers does not enter the picture; it also must not, for this would threaten to undercut the impartiality and impersonality of the rule of law.

According to Schmitt, normativists also have a certain idea of what things are like when there is order. When there is order then everything works according to plan. The normativist's paradigm of order is scheduled train traffic.[8] It is no coincidence that the latest and last offspring of positivist legal theory is Scott Shapiro's planning theory of law.[9] Schmitt had anticipated it as early as 1934.

The decisionist's idea of order is radically different. Order requires a power that precedes all norms. Hobbes' sovereign is the prime example.[10] Order is the opposite of insecurity and chaos. The power that creates order provides orientation by issuing commands, irrespective of whether these commands are of a general or special nature. Thus, the paradigmatic instance of law is the decision, not the rule that is equally applied in a plurality of cases. The decision emerges from the normative void. In relation to the chaos that it overcomes, its incidence is nothing short of miraculous.

---

[8] Schmitt, *Three Types*, n 1, 53.

[9] See SJ Shapiro, *Legality* (Cambridge, MA, Harvard University Press, 2013). Based on Jules Coleman's use of Michael Bratman's theory of collective agency, Shapiro develops a 'planning theory of law' (see J Coleman, *The Practice of Principle: In Defence of a Pragmatist Approach to Legal Theory* (Oxford, Oxford University Press, 2001); M Bratman, *Acting Together: A Planning Theory of Agency* (Oxford, Oxford University Press, 2014)).

[10] See T Hobbes, *Leviathan* (ed I Shapiro, New Haven, CT, Yale University Press, 2010).

## § 138

Neither Schmitt nor Dworkin believes that viewing the law as contingent combinations of rules and decisions – or of structures of commitment and freedom – is adequate to explain how legal knowledge is practised, more precisely, to explain what we do and what we invoke when we raise legal claims. If positivists and decisionists were right, the legal system would be a caricature or mockery of itself.

Evidently, the objection indicates that both Schmitt and Dworkin conceive of the reality of legal knowledge with regard to an ideal that it could possibly serve. According to Dworkin, this ideal is sufficient justification for coercion.[11] Of course, the quality of such justification depends on the moral arguments claimed in its support. At any rate, a mere combination of adherence to rules and intermittent haphazard choices appears to be entirely insufficient, at least if there is an alternative that articulates the reasons for the decision more clearly and transparently than the reference to rules plus discretion.

According to Dworkin, this alternative is already inherent in how courts justify decisions. Schmitt did not view this differently, even if his idea was more straightforwardly about sustaining a stratified order.

## § 139

According to Dworkin, a reasonably well-functioning legal system has no place, and must not have a place, for a decision in the Schmittian sense.

> *Decision in a Schmittian sense*: You have to stick to what I tell you to do, even if my choice may appear arbitrary or misguided.

In order to support his claim, Dworkin distinguishes three forms of discretion.[12] One encounters discretion in the weak sense, first, wherever arriving at a solution that involves exercising judgement. For example, whether or not a defect is to be considered 'gross' for the purpose of raising a warranty claim can only be determined by drawing on years of experience with defects of all kinds. The ability to muster this experience explains the power of judgement. Second, we can speak of discretion, again in a weak sense,

---

[11] See R Dworkin, *Law's Empire* (Cambridge, MA, Harvard University Press, 1986) 93.
[12] See Dworkin, n 7, 31–32.

where a court decides the issue, and there is no further avenue of appeal. The decision is then within the discretion of this court because it is not subject to any further review. But this does not mean that courts of final appeal are free to ignore the law. On the contrary, if they are smart, they engage in an effort to put the reasons for their decisions on the table as clearly as possible, given that they establish precedents for lower courts.

In both cases of discretion in the weak sense, constraints do not fall by the wayside, even if they have to be funnelled through the elusive medium of experienced judgement. Only completely unbound discretion would be discretion in a strong sense. If Dworkin is right, however, this third form of discretion must not exist in a legal system.

§ 140

From the perspective of Dworkin's project, analysing the exercise of judgement in decision making is the key to developing a credible alternative to legal positivism. His reflections conspicuously converge with what Schmitt calls 'thinking from within an established order'. It might be better, however, to refer to what Schmitt has in mind under the heading of 'institutional legal thinking'.

Dworkin demonstrates the constrained quality of discretion by using as an example a sergeant who is ordered to select five of his 'best people' for a mission.[13]

For outsiders, the term 'best people' may appear to be entirely indeterminate. Apparently, it does not provide us with any criteria for identifying those who are 'best'. Nevertheless, these criteria present themselves – they emerge from the background, as it were – when the problem of selection is perceived from within its own institutional context. It is possible to make sense of the term 'best people' if you are familiar with how a platoon operates. If you know the needs of military action, you can determine those who are the best people on the basis of their experience, tactical wisdom, prudence or physical strength.

Carl Schmitt has nothing else in mind when he speaks of 'concrete legal concepts'. One of the examples that he offers is indeed that of the 'brave soldier'.[14] In the tradition of European jurisprudence, it might have been

---

[13] See ibid 32.
[14] See Schmitt, *Three Types*, n 1, 55.

more apposite to recall the importance of the *bonus pater familias* as a yard-stick of diligent behaviour. But he wrote this in 1934.

> *The convict hangs motionless in his chair. He's still tied up. The child stands before him and is visibly unsure whether to touch him or not. From the background one hears the voice of the initiate:* A good prisoner sits still! *This is followed by resounding, hysterically irritated laughter.*

In order to produce legal knowledge, one must be familiar with the institutional context. That is the core message of all institutional legal thinking.

## § 141

One should not dismiss the category of 'concrete legal concepts' out of hand as right-wing absurdity simply because it was introduced by Schmitt in 1934. Undeniably, the most obnoxious part of Schmitt's text advocated the reinterpretation of existing law in light of the new institutional realities created by the Nazi takeover. He thereby set the stage for infusing existing legislation with new 'spirit', particularly in instances where this legislation used indeterminate language. Much harm was done by those who followed Schmitt's lead in practice. Hence, there is good reason to wear latex gloves when reading his theory.

Nevertheless, Schmitt misused what would under different circumstances easily pass as astute observation in order to serve an evil agenda. The core idea is not unsound. We face the external indeterminacy of legal terms everywhere. We encounter it in 'good business practice', in 'good faith', in 'danger to public safety' or in 'human dignity'. The category of concrete legal concepts is intended to capture the experience that the external indeterminacy of concepts disappears as soon as a participant in an institutional context makes internal statements from the perspective of the first-person plural. This is how 'we' see what matters. Owing to the fact that this is the perspective from which we state what we regard as valid, the reflexive use of the personal pronoun is usually omitted. We simply say what strikes us as right, as if it were perceived from the outside.

> *Poet*: With us. Here. Where we live. In our latitudes. Among honest merchants. It goes without saying.

> *Initiate*: It violates 'good faith' to claim that when a 'staircase' is ordered the handrail is not included.

In order to perceive as determinate what may strike outsiders as indeterminate we have to engage in what Kant called the 'extended way of thinking' (*erweiterte Denkungsart*).[15] What can be comprehended from the viewpoint of the first-person plural emerges from taking the positions of conceivable second-person singular that are assumed to imagine how matters are comprehended from the point of view of the first-person plural.

> *Pupil*: How would someone see it who wants to see how we all see it?

The verb that matters most is indeed that of 'seeing'. First of all, no concept in the sense of a list of criteria emerges from the use of concrete legal concepts. Their shape depends on the development of a view that is composed of partial aspects. The view itself is not fully conceptual. Certainly, more is at work than mere intuition, but it is essential that relevant components are viewed as parts of a view. It is the whole that explains the relevance of the parts. Nevertheless, this whole remains in an indeterminate state, even though its anticipation allows the various components to gather together.

> *Initiate*: Anyone who orders a 'staircase' associates a certain idea with the object. Only in exceptional cases, for example at the stairs of a castle weir, would the handrail be omitted. Moreover, for safety reasons alone it would be absurd to suppose that the customer wants to order a staircase without handrails. The fact that the customer has a choice when it comes to the design of the handrail does not detract from the fact that the handrail is included in the order of the 'staircase'.

By taking the perspective of someone who says what our view is, something that is originally only implicitly known is made explicit. In this way, it is possible to use a term without determining its elements conclusively. Rather, it can be explicated on the basis of a survey of particular instances of its use. The power of judgement seeks out what is general by moving from special case to special case, thereby determining the general *horizontally*.

---

[15] On the *erweiterte Denkungsart* – the expanded way of thinking – see I Kant, *Critique of the Power of Judgment* (trans P Guyer and E Matthews, Cambridge, Cambridge University Press, 2000). I only had the German version available: I Kant, *Kritik der Urteilskraft* (ed H Klemme, Hamburg, Meiner, 2009) B 137 pp 158–59. A superb guide to the *Critique* is M Chaouli, *Thinking with Kant's Critique of Judgment* (Cambridge, MA, Harvard University Press, 2017). The *erweiterte Denkungsart* plays a major role in H Arendt, *Lectures on Kant's Political Philosophy* (ed Ronald Beiner, Chicago, IL, University of Chicago Press, 1999).

It gives us a view of the general in particular instances, for example by comparing cases.

> *The judge steps in front of the unconscious convict and spreads her legs over the chair. She pulls up her skirt and says to the convict*: 'Well?'

According to Dworkin, principles are among the standards with which the power of judgement operates in order to determine how we view matters. Principles have weight (see § 131). How much of it they have depends on the situation. The weight reveals itself in the situation, although it cannot merely be intuited; it requires an exchange of arguments. Nonetheless, the weight of principles is essentially situation dependent. Schmitt would agree.

Dworkin[16] believes that the unquestionable relevance of principles indicates two things. First, the law is not a system of rules. Second, in hard cases the relevance of arguments about principles shows that the law is embedded in morality.

§ 142

In his early work, Dworkin differentiates between principles and policies.[17] Principles establish rights and indicate what is owed to individuals. Policies are not individualised. They are about what is considered desirable in the aggregate. They do not give rise to legal claims.

> *Politician*: We need elite universities, flexible labour markets and open borders.

According to Dworkin, principles are trump cards that ordinarily override the pursuit of policies in the context of legal decision making. In order to understand why policies are weaker than rights, one simply has to attempt to translate them into rights. One can then immediately see why they are too weak to give rise to a legally enforceable claim.

> *Pupil*: I have the right to a university degree.
>
> *Initiate*: This is an extremely weak right – so weak that it is actually no right at all. For, on the one hand, it is not guaranteed by the

---

[16] Ronald Dworkin's two works that continue to be the best introduction to his legal thinking are the books cited in nn 7 and 11. For an introduction, see S Guest, *Ronald Dworkin*, 3rd edn (Stanford, CA, Stanford University Press, 2012) and A Ripstein (ed), *Ronald Dworkin* (Cambridge, Cambridge University Press, 2007). See also S Hershovitz (ed), *Exploring Law's Empire, The Jurisprudence of Ronald Dworkin* (Oxford, Oxford University Press, 2006). Dworkin's last major and rather enigmatic work is *Justice for Hedgehogs* (Cambridge, MA, Harvard University Press, 2013).

[17] See, in particular, 'Hard Cases' in Dworkin, n 7, 81–130.

constitution and, on the other, a lot of leeway must be left to legislation for its implementation. You can't just go to court and claim your doctorate.

The alleged right to a university degree is therefore at best a policy objective. This does not mean that it is meaningless. It means that good government should aim at increasing the number of graduates with a university degree.

§ 143

Like no other legal theorist before or after him, Dworkin places morally significant 'theories' at the centre of legal knowledge. In his view, the existence of a right and its threshold weight in relation to other rights or political objectives must be determined from within a 'theory of rights'. But this is not the only theory that matters. The connection to positive law is established, for example, by the best possible theory of law or, concurringly, by various best possible theories of a cluster of rights and obligations.

Legal validity is, therefore, in Dworkin's view not anchored in a social rule, but an effect of a variety of overlapping theories. Owing to this deep theory-dependence, the legal system, as a social institution, functions like a bundle of concurring opinions.

According to Dworkin, a theory of rights is implicit in every justification of a legal claim. Dworkin is, in principle, open-minded when it comes to elaborating such a theory. It is conceivable to develop it on a utilitarian or a deontological basis, even though he leans strongly toward the latter.

> *Author:* Utilitarian theories[18] focus on the overall balance of preference satisfaction. If the balance is improved through the addition of an individual right, then this right ought to exist. Deontological theories, by contrast, ask what treatment is due to human beings regardless of whether how they are treated has a positive or negative effect on the overall balance of preference satisfaction.

Dworkin himself developed in his earlier work a theory that focuses on a fundamental right to equal respect and concern.[19] Only in his later work has human dignity taken centre stage.[20]

---

[18] For an introduction, see I Shapiro, *The Moral Foundations of Politics* (New Haven, CT, Yale University Press, 2003) 18–70.

[19] See Dworkin, n 7, 180–83, 272–78.

[20] See Dworkin, n 16, 14, 255.

## § 144

Dworkin believes that any theory of rights must employ at least two distinctions.[21]

One distinction concerns the difference between abstract and concrete rights. Rights are abstract in the format in which we encounter them, for example in a charter of fundamental rights. By contrast, rights are concrete if their scope and content have already been articulated in relation to public interests in a number of cases.

> *Judge*: Wearing a headscarf for the purpose of signalling membership in a religious or ethnic group is in principle protected by the right to have one's private life respected and by freedom of worship. The legislature, however, does not violate its obligation to protect the exercise of these rights if it allows employers to demand the removal of a headscarf in order to facilitate trustful dealings with customers in a commercial setting.

Of greater importance is the other distinction. It concerns institutional rights and moral background rights. The former rights are either laid down in legislation or recognised in case law. The latter rights are elements of a theory that states what rights people ought to have on moral grounds.

Institutional rights have more weight than moral background rights.

## § 145

But why? Why can we not take it for granted that the rights contained in the Universal Declaration of Human Rights are applicable even if a country's constitution only partially recognises these rights or does not recognise them at all? If a theory of rights reaches the conclusion that the rights of the Universal Declaration are exactly the rights that everyone should enjoy, then those rights should be protected everywhere.

Would there be anything wrong with that?

In order to answer the question of whether the moral theory of rights alone should determine our rights, this theory must be supplemented by an overall theory of law. Only such a theory can explain why positive law not only matters, but also substantially limits the relevance of moral demands.

---

[21] See Dworkin, n 7, 93, 101.

According to Dworkin, the importance of sticking to positive law is based primarily on viewing it as the answer to the question under what conditions someone may legitimately be subject to coercion. One of these conditions is that persons facing the prospect of being coerced by another must be able to anticipate the use of force. The standard, which is forcibly enforced, must not simply be made up at the moment of enforcement. Now, according to Dworkin, it may well be the case that the existence of a right can be established on moral grounds only. But moral judgement is not always uncontroversial. That explains, again, why positive law matters. It establishes a certain degree of legal certainty. In addition, positive law realises and gives life to morally significant demands, such as those for democratic self-determination and political participation. Hence, there are good moral reasons for taking positive law seriously.

But these are not the only reasons why the decision of legal issues must not simply rely on the soundest theory of moral rights. According to Dworkin, one is obligated to follow positive law owing to one's membership in a political community. This obligation is a subset of 'associative obligations' that arise from cooperation (for example among colleagues) or a close relationship (for example between friends). These relationships 'attract' obligation even though the participants have never made any explicit pledges.[22]

§ 146

The theory of law therefore requires the theory of rights to match the positive laws of a particular community. The interpretive elaboration of individual legal claims thus acquires two dimensions:[23] the dimension of 'fit' in the sense that a morally substantiated justification and interpretation of rights must be compatible, at least to a large extent, with positive legal materials; and the dimension of moral justification in the context of which an effort must be made to provide the best possible moral justification of positive law. Arguably, such a justification will invariably bear a particular cultural imprint. Unsurprisingly, according to Dworkin, all theories of rights and even all theories of law are particulars.[24]

The demand for the best possible justification sounds like the call for a blatant apology of the status quo. The underlying idea is, however,

---

[22] See Dworkin, n 11, 185–202.
[23] See Dworkin, n 7, 107.
[24] See Dworkin, n 11, 411–13.

quite plausible. What is at stake is the justification of coercion. The coercive act must abide by positive law. From the moral justification requirement follows, however, that positive law ought to be cast in the best possible moral light. Otherwise the justification of coercion would fail. Practices of coercion may only continue if we can put them – the constraints of institutional history notwithstanding – on the most morally appealing base.

Against this background, Dworkin's highly controversial insistence on the one 'right answer' appears to make sense. There can only be one answer to the question whether someone has a legal claim (or obligation). From the point of view of both the theories of law and rights, this answer must be unequivocal. For it would be utterly frivolous to point out to a convict that it is a matter of luck whether or not he will be convicted, or that this depends on the judge's whims. The justification requirement would not be met.

> *The curtain rises. One sees a bare, windowless room, poorly illuminated by neon light. The inscription 'suum cuique retribuere' in the middle of the wall has been emblazoned with a stencil. The judge steps out of the darkness and stands in front of the convict, who lies in the right corner of the room. The convict is still wearing a bandage around his head, which is now showing blood stains. Judge: That's the only right answer.*

According to Dworkin, from the point of view of the theory of law, that theory of rights is more persuasive which better matches with the existing legal materials.

But this 'fit' can never be perfect, in particular not in the context of the common law. The reason for this is that common law has the built-in propensity to render itself periodically obscure through the accumulation of an ever-growing number of precedents distinguished by barely perceptible differences. Over time, the law turns out to be so complex that it becomes next to impossible to find one's way. Moreover, some precedents are likely to be inconsistent with others. At a certain point, it becomes necessary to identify 'bad' law and let go of it. How large the margin of tolerance is, is a question to which the theories of law and rights should be prepared to give an answer.

## § 147

Our discussion of concrete legal terms has stopped with the recognition that the decision-making process takes place against the backdrop of an institutional context that encompasses 'views' of what counts as right or wrong behaviour. Such views concern, for example, the fair treatment of contracting parties or the procedure that the police ought to follow in the course of an interrogation. Normative standards with 'weight' play an important role in articulating these understandings.

But views are not concepts, and in the long term one cannot rest content with developing mere views. The common sense that conveys a common view quickly comes to an end. The level of intuitive judgement must then be left behind and give room to discursive conceptualisation. Dworkin used the term 'conceptions' for the results of more elaborate and tentatively creative attempts to determine the meaning of concepts.[25]

Dworkin explains what he has in mind by using another instructive example. A chess game referee is confronted with the question whether it violates the etiquette of chess for one player to irritate the other with a penetrating stupid grin. In order to answer this question, for which no explicit standard can be found in the rule book, the referee must develop a conception of chess. To achieve this, she has to ask herself which human abilities are decisive for the success of the game. Should only cool intelligence count or also toughness or a modicum of ability to manipulate? Whatever the referee's answer might be, she will have to develop a conception of chess that is clearer and more specific than the previously shared view. Such a conception will then be incorporated into the working of the institution because it helps close a gap that has existed in the etiquette so far. The conception of the whole – of the meaning and purpose of the game as such – feeds back into the institutional practice and allows a part of the whole to be supplemented. The whole – the institution of the game of chess – creates in someone who participates in the institutional practice a conception of itself and of what lends authority to its rules in order to arrive at a better understanding of itself. This is the life of objective spirit.

In somewhat similar terms, Dworkin presents this matter – of course, without elusive allusions to classical German philosophy – in his early work. He will later come to present the same process under the name of 'constructive interpretation'. An interpretation of this kind contains a creative element. It suggests that its object serves a purpose and strives to make

---

[25] See ibid 70–72.

it look particularly good in light of this purpose. Dworkin even claims that interpretations should aim at presenting the object as the best of its genre or kind.

## § 148

With these processes in mind, Dworkin conceives of the law generally as a self-reflective process of constructive interpretation. Law operates on the basis of an understanding – a conception – that it develops about itself.

It thus turns out to be, indeed, objective spirit. As an institution law is what it is by creating accounts of itself and using them to recalibrate institutional practice. Its operation involves developing a conception of its point and of what gives it authority. The chess example demonstrates that the objectification of spirit is carried out when the chess game referee closes the gap in the rules after she has reflected on the meaning and purpose of the game. This is what the objective quality of spirit is all about. The further institutional practice of the game is based on a conception developed as the practice is represented by the referee.

The theory of rights, which was mentioned earlier, does nothing else in relation to positive law. The dimension of moral idealisation stems from a constructive effort of interpretation, which is supposed to lend a morally appealing appearance to positive law. Ultimately, the theory of law is nothing more than a constructive self-interpretation of the practice of solving legal problems that are tied, ultimately, to the task of justifying coercion.

## § 149

Dworkin distinguished three candidates for the constructive self-interpretation of legal practice as a whole:[26] conventionalism (Dworkin's name for late positivism), pragmatism (Dworkin's name for American legal realism), and his own conception of law, namely 'law as integrity'. After an in-depth analysis, Dworkin finds that neither conventionalism nor pragmatism fit legal practice. It is in this context that his arguments against discretion in the strong sense and for the relevance of positive law return.

---

[26] See Dworkin, note 11.

The basic idea underlying 'law as integrity' is a general principle of equal treatment that is rooted in the right to equal respect and concern. According to Dworkin, integrity demands that positive law be interpreted such that it can be seen as permeated by a coherent scheme of principles.

Since the development of such a scheme requires superhuman intellectual capacities, Dworkin invents a superhuman judge named 'Hercules' who is capable of carrying out this task. Once Hercules is finished with it, the law amounts to a coherent system that excludes any arbitrariness in the application of rules to facts. It would speak with one voice to all and express the political community's common will:

> [Integrity] ... requires government to speak with one voice, to act in a principled and coherent manner toward all its citizens, to extend to everyone the substantive standards of justice and fairness it uses for some.

> According to law as integrity propositions of law are true if they figure in or follow from the principles of justice, fairness, and procedural due process that provide the best constructive interpretation of the community's legal practice.

> [A] Citizen cannot treat himself as the author of a collection of laws that are inconsistent in principle, nor can he see that collection as sponsored by any Rousseauian general will.[27]

## § 150

Dworkin's early reflections on the relation between rules and principles have been well received and productively used in German legal theory. Robert Alexy, who modified Dworkin's theory of principles and transplanted it into Jürgen Habermas' discourse theory,[28] deserves special mention.

According to Alexy, principles are optimisation rules.[29] Their relative weight is determined in the process of balancing. Balancing is subject to a

---

[27] ibid 165, 225, 198.

[28] See R Alexy, *A Theory of Legal Argumentation: The Theory of Rational Discourse as Theory of Legal Justification* (trans R Adler and N MacCormick, Oxford, Oxford University Press, 1989).

[29] Robert Alexy's main work is his *A Theory of Constitutional Rights* (trans J Rivers, New York, Oxford University Press, 2002). For introductions, see G Pavlakos (ed), *Law, Rights and Discourse: The Legal Philosophy of Robert Alexy* (Oxford, Hart Publishing, 2007) and M Klatt (ed), *Institutionalized Reason: The Jurisprudence of Robert Alexy* (Oxford, Oxford University Press, 2012). For a contrasting approach, see K Günther, *The Sense of Appropriateness: Application Discourses in Morality and Law* (trans J Farrell, Albany, NY, State University of New York Press, 1993).

formal requirement. One principle must only yield to another if the importance of the realisation of the latter is greater than the intensity of the impairment of the former.

> *Alexy (to the author)*: This can be stated more precisely, Mr Somek: the higher the degree of non-fulfilment or impairment of one principle, the greater the importance of the fulfilment of the other has to be.

Balancing decisions ought to be arrived at in practical discourses, which are informal procedures for the argumentative justification of norms. Ideally, they are characterised by communications that are free of domination or asymmetries of power. The participants in an exchange of arguments share the goal of reaching an agreement on what is supposedly the right solution.

Habermas developed the theory of discourse that Alexy adopted for legal argumentation. An objection to Alexy's thesis that legal discourse is a special case of practical discourse originated from Habermas' circle. According to Klaus Günther, legal discourses are best conceived of as application discourses.[30] Their point is not the justification or rejection of norms; rather, it lies in determining their appropriate application.

## § 151

'Incorporation' is the concept designating one of the major developments in Anglo-American legal positivism over the last few decades. It may well have been triggered by the fact that Dworkin's theories of law and legal reasoning are quite congenial to the style of legal analysis that we associate with the common law. While legal positivism talks about rules as though law was made up of statutes, Dworkin has many illuminating things to say about precedents and about the use, by courts, of arguments with significant moral or political import. If one juxtaposes the legal philosophies of H.L.A. Hart and Dworkin, the former appears to be somewhat skimpy, dry and detached from the law as it is practised. For this reason, possibly, legal positivism may have developed the desire to demonstrate its ability that it can account, too, for the wealth of legal arguments that is manifest in court opinions.

---

[30] K Günther, *The Sense of Appropriateness: Application Discourses in Morality and Law* (trans J Farrell, Albany, NY, State University of New York Press, 1993).

The idea underlying this move is that the law can – within the rule of recognition – incorporate morality as a source of law.[31] Hence, principles and policies can be regarded as part of the legal system based on a rule that is accepted and socially practised by legal officials for the purpose of determining valid law. One may want to ask, of course, whether what is thus incorporated is merely the principles that are actually referred to by courts in their case law or whether incorporation can actually extend to appeals to morality as such. This would imply, then, that incorporation invests judges with the power to complement legal analysis with moral arguments that they deem to be convincing by their own lights. Indeed, some 'inclusive legal positivists' have argued that incorporation can concern morality *tout court*. Consequently, any substantive matter could then be decided on the grounds of what judges believe to be the most persuasive moral grounds.

It should be noted that inclusive legal positivism amounts to a stark departure from Kelsen's project. Not that Kelsen would have objected to judges resolving legal issues on moral grounds, at least so long as they stay within the scope of their discretion, but he would have drawn a sharp line between the interpretation of legal norms and the exercise of such discretion authorised by procedural rules. Inclusive legal positivists would view the pursuit of moral excellence as legal obligation if the rule of recognition said so. For Kelsen this could never be taken at face value, for morality is not rational.

§ 152

Joseph Raz remains unconvinced. He endorses 'exclusive' legal positivism.[32] This label seems to suggest that Raz is opposed to incorporating morality into the law in order to keep the law pure. But this would not at all capture his position. His approach is far more subtle. In his view, if there were no positive law, judges would simply decide cases on moral grounds. The existence of the law alters this situation. It pushes moral reasons aside by excluding, if perhaps only partly, their relevance for legal decision making.

---

[31] See, for example, W Waluchow, 'Legal positivism, inclusive versus exclusive' in *Routledge Encyclopedia of Philosophy*, www.rep.routledge.com/articles/thematic/legal-positivism-inclusive-versus-exclusive/v-1/sections/inclusive-and-exclusive-positivism.

[32] For an introduction see 'Incorporation by Law' in his *Between Authority and Interpretation: On the Theory of Law and Practical Reason* (Oxford, Oxford University Press, 2009) 182–202.

Raz concludes, therefore, that it is rather odd to believe, as the 'incorporationists' ostensibly do, that the law incorporates morality in the second round after excluding it in the first. The core claim of exclusive legal positivism is that the law excludes morality, and the question to ask is to what extent it actually does so. If the law explicitly refers to a moral standard, such as a standard of common decency, it does not make it its own. It yields to and possibly even modifies morality. But the situation is in principle not different from cases in which a conflict of laws statute says that in certain cases the law of another country has to be applied. The legal system makes room for another system – or cedes ground to it – without making it part of its own.

## § 153

It is not easy to see why and how Raz's exclusive legal positivism is still part of the larger positivist agenda. In his view, the legitimacy of law needs to be spelled out in moral terms. Existing law, at any rate, is of moral significance, because what it claims overlaps partly with the scope of moral reasons. De facto the law tells us what we ought to do for the reason of respecting others, behaving fairly, and contributing to the common good.

The moral legitimacy that the law *claims* for itself does not, however, in and of itself also invest it with this quality. Hence, it must be possible to distinguish between statements that say what the law claims and other statements that ascertain what our moral obligations truly are. But how can we draw this distinction without denying the law's membership of the moral domain?

One might suggest that law and morality give us different 'aspects' of what our obligations are. Yet, the difference between law and morality is not comparable to the difference between economic and aesthetic perspectives on a certain subject. A building may be energy efficient, but still ugly. In a similar vein, one might claim that a law is valid, but morally too wicked to be obeyed. Raz does not find such a differentiation of perspectives convincing. In his view, law and morality do not give us different aspects of a subject matter. They are about one and the same thing, namely what our rights and our obligations are. The difference between statements of our duties and statements of what the law claims our duties to be is anchored in the difference between detached 'standpoint' statements and those for which such a detachment is impossible.

Standpoint statements speak from some particular point of view without involving a commitment to its adequacy. We can say what the law is without shouldering responsibility for the content of that statement by speaking from a point of view:

> *Initiate*: According to canon law, married couples cannot obtain a divorce.

In a like manner we can state what the law requires from the standpoint of the 'legal man' without thereby claiming that what we say is indeed an account of our obligations.

> *Pupil*: Legally speaking, Roman Catholics are married forever.

Such a detachment is possible because the law only de facto claims to possess authority. It is a fact that the law's claim to authority is based on beliefs in certain reasons, but this does not commit anyone to believing that such apparent reasons are also real.

Standpoint statements are impossible, by contrast, in the case of valid reason. 'Valid reasons', Raz explains, 'are real reasons, and once you have committed yourself that you are talking about valid reasons, you can no longer say "but I do not know if there is any reason to do so"'. Hence, detached statements are inconsistent morality: 'Morality is another perspective reference to which one (?) cannot be used to suspend truth'.[33]

§ 154

*The room from before. A cleaning person sweeps up the floor. Otherwise the room is empty. When sweeping up, a piece of bandage flutters up.*

---

[33] ibid 186.

# Rupture

## § 155

*Child*: Mom, I'm so sad.

*Mother*: But why, my dear?

*Child*: I can't make up my mind.

*Mother*: Be happy about this! That's how you are staying a good person. As long as you don't decide and don't act, you can't do anything wrong.

## § 156

According to Ronald Dworkin, the authority of law is mediated by those morally significant principles that cast laws and authoritative precedents in the most appealing light. Expressing this idea in the language of German jurisprudence, this means that the authority of law is founded on those 'values' that tie the law together 'from within' (they comprise the so-called 'internal system' of law, see § 58 on Heck).

> *Initiate (to the pupil)*: Freedom of contract – ie the right to decide for oneself with whom one would like to enter into an agreement – realises and gives life to the principle of private autonomy. But the scope of application of this principle is not unlimited. It is counterbalanced by another principle demanding that access to important goods be available for everyone. Freedom of contract must therefore yield to this other principle in the event that someone happens to be the only provider of an important good. Depending on the importance of the good and its availability from other sources, the provider may be either obligated to sell and to provide access to these goods to everyone or prohibited from differentiating inappropriately between those who request them. Discrimination based on race, gender or sexual orientation would be instances of inappropriate differentiation. Hence, we arrive at a scheme of three principles. Here private autonomy, there the principle of access, and the ban on discrimination in the middle.

*Pupil*: The law has integrity if this scheme is sustained without inappropriate exceptions, which would be made, for example, if discrimination bans only applied to access to the labour market and not to the employment relation itself.

*Initiate*: That's it!

Such a scheme can be worked out by accepting as a premise that there are right answers to questions of balancing. Only on that basis is it possible to establish well-founded and stable relations between principles.

*Initiate*: If there were no correct answer, it would be left to chance whether the employment relationship must also be subject to protection against discrimination. The scheme would disintegrate.

Dworkin's theory thus envisages a positive system of legal knowledge. It is positive insofar as it promises to generate satisfactory answers for all issues. The answer is never negative in the sense that we are left clueless as to what it might be.

*Child*: But I don't know what's right.

## § 157

Objections can be raised against the idea that such a positive system is possible. They begin at the point where the idea is most vulnerable, namely the conviction that the system can and must determine the legal rule that is to be applied in a certain case. A positive system would not be possible if there were no answer to this question. The relations of relative priority between and among principles ('in these cases private autonomy, in those the access principle') would remain indeterminate.

The system (Dworkin's 'scheme') is nothing but a network of such priority relations.

Throughout his long career, Dworkin defended the view that there are objectively correct answers to moral and legal questions. Therefore, in his view, there must also be a correct answer to the question of which legal rule is appropriate to apply to which type of case.

Dworkin's critics do not have to reject moral objectivity to express doubts about whether it is necessary or even only advisable to root legal knowledge in moral correctness. Jeremy Waldron pointed out perceptively that even if there could or must be a right answer, it may de facto remain unclear what it is simply because the matter remains controversial, at least for the time being.[1] It is not inconceivable that people will have persistent differences over questions of morality. Indeed, it is to be expected, especially since – unlike in the empirical sciences – the methods for supporting statements are notoriously controversial, too. After all, there are different schools of moral philosophy and the divergence of approaches among these schools persists. It is therefore better, according to Waldron, to place the existence of decision-making powers at the centre of a theory of law and not the correct answer to substantive moral questions.

What is more, if the ambition to discover the correct answer dominates judicial decision making, legal certainty is likely taking its toll. In the common law context, at any rate, the reasons for decisions fragment into various concurring opinions in which peacocky judges exhibit their idiosyncratic perspectives on what they consider to be correct.

§ 158

Worse still, Dworkin appears to underappreciate the complexity of moral problems. This may explain why he does not take incommensurability into account.[2]

Two principles are incommensurable if neither is superior to the other, while they are also not equally significant. There is no common scale available to determine their relative value or weight.

> *Mother*: Look, there is someone working on an oil-painting right in the middle of the intersection. This cannot be right.

> *Child*: I don't know what's right. I'm totally stuck because I can't engage in balancing. I find it impossible to express impairments of artistic freedom in gains to public safety. One value cannot be translated into the other.

In order to make balancing rationally intelligible, it is conceivable to measure the weight of principles in certain situations according to the principle's

---

[1] Waldron's critical examination of the 'right answer thesis' can be found in J Waldron, 'The Irrelevance of Moral Objectivity' in his *Law and Disagreement* (Oxford, Oxford University Press, 1999) 164–87.

[2] The following discussion of incommensurability is obviously indebted to J Raz, *The Morality of Freedom* (Oxford, Clarendon Press, 1986). See also R Chang, *Incommensurability, Incomparability, and Practical Reason* (Cambridge, MA, Harvard University Press, 1997).

own internal scale and to compare the intensity of impairments and realisations not directly between, but, in the first round, from within each principle. A mild restriction of artistic freedom – for example, an exception for certain places – may then seem justified in view of the sizable gain in public safety.

> *Textbook example*: A ban on working on a painting in the middle of a busy intersection is a slight restriction on artistic freedom because there remain many conceivable other places for its exercise. The increase in road safety, by contrast, is considerable. The scale of balancing moves towards the latter.

This perspective on the intensity of impairments or realisations of each principle ignores the fact that the comparison again requires a common baseline. It cannot be taken for granted that public safety and artistic freedom would be of the same value or the same weight even if they were fully realised. This is exactly the premise challenged by the incommensurability thesis. One cannot turn what is incommensurable into something commensurable so long as it remains unclear whether the goods in question are equivalent or one of them is of disproportionately greater value.

§ 159

Nor does Dworkin envisage tragic conflicts.[3] Conflicts of this kind involve two competing moral authorities whose demands are equally compelling and yet incompatible.

The classic example is the conflict between family duty and loyalty to the political community. The story of Antigone, who wants to bury her brother according to a religious rite in spite of the King of Thebes' prohibition, is the paradigmatic example of this type of conflict. There is no moral norm available for the resolution of a tragic collision. Each action approved by one authority is disapproved by the other.

The tragic conflict can only disappear if the affected person somehow perishes in it – either through her death or through a transformation. Such metamorphoses are bearable – and somewhat intelligible – only in the medium of art. Aesthetic experience gives us access to the conflict without

---

[3] The most impressive forays into our understanding of tragic conflicts and their return in the context of law are the works by Christoph Menke. See above all his *Tragödie im Sittlichen: Recht und Gerechtigkeit nach Hegel* (Frankfurt aM, Suhrkamp, 1996) and *Tragic Play: Irony and Theater from Sophocles to Beckett* (trans J Phillips, New York, Columbia University Press, 2009).

making us suffer through it. The narrator occupies the morally indeterminate position from which the conflict can be resolved without arriving at a conclusion in moral terms. The aesthetic alternative to the right answer is the ending. With the ending we encounter the harshness of life.

Art thus opens up a dimension of human experience that is inaccessible to moral judgement. It enables us to see situations of human failure as situations that are incompatible with action. We can face up to such failure only if we suspend practice and escape to the world of fiction. In this world, matters are no longer serious. They become bearable not because the problem has been solved; rather, we can risk getting immersed in it owing to our detachment. We can look crushing predicaments in the eye in the medium of aesthetic appearances. By exiting into the fictional world we replace the relevance of moral norms with standards of aesthetic success. We can relate to what is too large for us by enjoying how well a plot is hewn or a story staged. Remarkably, what is well narrated can thus take the place of the good.

The thesis that there must be a correct answer to all moral questions turns out to be aesthetically shallow. Bluntly speaking, it is tasteless. But it is widespread. Many people read literary works in search of a moral message. Some even write such works in order to articulate moral ideas. It must be questioned whether they thereby severely underachieve what can be accomplished in art.

§ 160

The aesthetic objection to the belief in the relevance of moral insight for legal knowledge is cognate to what is perhaps the most basic contention of so-called Critical Legal Studies.[4]

Critical Legal Studies originated in the 1970s in the United States.[5] They quickly became a forum for legal scholars and practising lawyers who considered themselves to be progressive or 'on the left'. By the late 1980s, the steam was already out of the movement. Nevertheless, there are still representatives of Critical Legal Studies in the United States today, especially

---

[4] An anthology of important contributions to *Critical Legal Studies* was published by AC Hutchinson (Totowa, NJ, Rowman and Littlefield, 1988); and the best introduction, despite the strong emphasis on law and economics, remains M Kelman, *A Guide to Critical Legal Studies* (Cambridge, MA, Harvard University Press, 1988). A very concise introduction that is followed by a sketch of the author's own social theory is RM Unger, *The Critical Legal Studies Movement* (Cambridge, MA, Harvard University Press, 1986), 2nd edn with the subtitle *Another Time, A Greater Task* (London, Verso, 2015).

[5] See M Tushnet, 'Critical Legal Studies: A Political History' (1991) 100 *Yale Law Journal* 1515–44.

at Harvard Law School. They are now appealing to an international student body. However, these are only weak reverberations of what went on before. The faculty controversies in the heyday of the movement in the early to mid 1980s earned Harvard Law School the reputation of being the 'Beirut of legal education'.

This is all over now.

## § 161

The Critical Legal Studies movement can most easily be introduced by looking at two of its leading figures: Duncan Kennedy[6] and Roberto Mangabeira Unger.[7] In different ways, both emphasise the indeterminacy of law. Kennedy does so with his unconventional perspective of the rational undecidability of legal questions and Unger with his refusal to recognise any social arrangement as the only conceivable realisation of the values of freedom and equality. In Unger's view, all institutional arrangements contain slight and marginal variations that might serve as means of making potentially radical transformations. Their realisation would never require a revolution in the sense of totally changing the entire institutional context for social life.

Both Kennedy and Unger choose the same basic social experience as their point of departure. An insoluble human conflict is reflected in the legal materials: our organised legal relations are just as necessary for the realisation of our freedom as they render it impossible. This simultaneity of necessity and impossibility is a manifestation of the 'fundamental contradiction' of our social existence:

> *Duncan Kennedy (without beard and glasses)*: … the goal of individual freedom is at the same time dependent on and incompatible with the communal coercive action that is necessary to achieve it.[8]

---

[6] Two contributions by Duncan Kennedy are essential to the rise of Critical Legal Studies: 'Form and Substance in Private Law Adjudication' (1976) 89 *Harvard Law Review* 1685–778, and 'The Structure of Blackstone's Commentaries' (1979) 28 *Buffalo Law Review* 205–382. A small selection of Kennedy's legal theoretical writings is now available under the title *Legal Reasoning: Collected Essays* (Aurora, Davies Group Publishers, 2008); his rather labyrinthine major work is *A Critique of Adjudication. Fin de Siecle*, Cambridge, MA, Harvard University Press, 1997).

[7] The most seminal work of the movement appears to have been RM Unger, *Knowledge and Politics* (New York, Free Press, 1975). Unger's most extensive elaboration of this social theory is still *False Necessity: Anti-Necessitarian Social Theory in the Service of Radical Democracy* (Cambridge, Cambridge University Press, 1988).

[8] Kennedy, 'Structure', n 6, 211.

This incompatibility affects not only the legal materials but also the legal knowledge with which we account for them:

> *Duncan Kennedy (from a pulpit)*: The fundamental contradiction – that relations with others are both necessary to and incompatible with our freedom – is not only intense. It is also pervasive. First, it is an aspect of our experience of every form of social life …. Second, within law, as law is commonly defined, it is not just an aspect, but the very essence of every problem.[9]

Unger grasps the same thought by casting it as the elementary conflict of the two enabling conditions of human self-realisation. These consist of 'the need to participate in group life and the effort to avoid the dangers of subjugation and depersonalization that attend such engagement'.[10]

## § 162

Kennedy tries to demonstrate that the fundamental contradiction is replicated in the internal contractions of all attempts to overcome it. The ideology that he addresses for the purpose of demonstration is 'liberalism'.

The early writings of both Kennedy and Unger unsurprisingly speak to liberalism's embrace of individual freedom. It is manifest in the celebration of individual rights and of legal rules that promise to be neutral among different conceptions of the good life. They claim that liberalism's promise to have discovered the model of society that reconciles individual freedom with the strains of social commitments is false. The falsity of this promise explains why liberalism is, in their view, ideological. Liberalism glosses over the internal tensions of law. The reality of the legal system becomes hidden underneath an apologetic sugar coating of idealisations. In the end, law dressed up in liberal garb is itself merely an ideology.

## § 163

The originality of Kennedy's approach lies in locating the 'clash' of 'enabling conditions of self-assertion'[11] within legal reasoning, thus formulating a legal theory for an unreconciled society.

---

[9] ibid 213.
[10] RM Unger, *Passion: An Essay on Personality* (New York, Free Press, 1984) 35–36.
[11] ibid 21.

According to Kennedy, the fundamental contradiction reveals itself in recurring and unresolved conflicts between ethical types of legal arguments. In his early and famous essay on 'Form and Substance in Private Law Adjudication', Kennedy pinpoints 'individualistic' and 'altruistic' ways of thinking in private law. Individualism is entirely consistent with liberal ideology, altruism with what liberalism invariably has to accept as a supplement without producing an appropriate way of accounting for it. Kennedy presents the tension by pointing out that favouring clear rules and adherence to the literal meanings of words are typically individualistic, while operating with open standards such as 'good faith' or situation-sensitive balancing is indicative of altruism. His observations give rise to the claim that although individualism dominates the American common law of contracts, this dominance is always mitigated by the inclusion of altruistic motives. None of the spontaneously occurring shifts between the ethical model as used in legal discourse is based on any of the models involved. It is always a political choice. This is how we encounter the fundamental contradiction. The path that the legal arguments follow involves ultimately pure, 'existential' leaps.

This conviction earned Kennedy the nickname 'Critical Legal Sartre'. Pierre Schlag, whose work, if space were to permit it, would merit a separate chapter, is responsible for this appellation.[12]

## § 164

'All law is politics'. This catchy slogan of Critical Legal Studies conceals the subtlety of the approach at least as much as the attempt to embellish it with profound-sounding existentialist window dressing. Kennedy basically reconstructs a negative system of legal knowledge that operates complementarily to the positive system. This is, indeed, a remarkable perspective.

The positive system is the correlate of the belief in an always possible right answer. As a result of the aggregation and ordering of right answers, a system emerges that consists of priority relations of principles in relation to various types of situations. Eventually, the law is determinate.

The negative system is the correlate of the disbelief in right answers. Such an answer is unavailable because it is always equally possible to pursue the individualistic or the altruistic path of argumentation. The law is

---

[12] See P Schlag, 'The Problem of the Subject' (1991) 69 *Texas Law Review* 1627–743, 1679.

indeterminate. It is indeterminate not only here or there or at the margins, but it is indeterminate at its core. It obtains determinacy only owing to an external influence. This external factor is the political decision. Owing to this relationship of determination, what is external to the law turns out to be its essence. Law is politics. The law is with itself only when it is outside of itself.

The negative system is not simply the negation of the positive system. It is a reminder of the impossibility of the positive system that escorts it like a shadow. The impossibility is its essence, while that of which it is the essence is mere semblance. The positive system seems to exist. Seeming is its mode of existence.

Kennedy's former student Jack Balkin has – much to his credit – elaborated the relation between the positive and the negative system in a manner that is both razor sharp and 'crystal-clear'.[13]

## § 165

In Balkin's view, legal knowledge amounts to a series of decisions linking rules with factual situations to which they apply (he calls these decisions 'rule-choices'). Indeed, engaging in these decisions is what the formation of a system amounts to.

An example taken from Balkin's analysis of Kennedy's tort law materials illustrates how this works. Similar to Kennedy, Balkin distinguishes between two ethical models, 'individualism', on the one hand, and 'communalism', on the other.

> *The stage is empty and gloomy. You think you see movement in the background, but it's too dark to perceive anything clearly.*
>
> *Author:* Why is anyone not doing anything?
>
> *Voice (from the dark):* It's so thrilling! We are listening. *(Laughter)*

---

[13] The following of Jack Balkin's works deserve special mention: 'The Crystalline Structure of Legal Thought' (1986) 39 *Rutgers Law Review* 1–110; 'Deconstructive Practice and Legal Theory' (1987) 96 *Yale Law Journal* 743–86; 'Taking Ideology Seriously: Ronald Dworkin and the CLS Critique' (1987) 55 *University of Missouri Kansas City Law Review* 392–433. For a deconstructive criticism of Balkin's ideas see P Schlag, '"Le Hors de Texte, C'est Moi". The Politics of Form and the Domestication of Deconstruction' (1990) 11 *Cardozo Law Review* 1631–74.

*The author shrugs his shoulders and rolls his shoulders to release his neck
tension a little. He says to himself:* Does it have to be? It has to be!
*The light goes out. Immediately afterwards the clattering of a keyboard
can be heard.*

Individualism favours freedom. Consequently, it tends to minimise responsibility. Communalism favours solidarity, which explains why it tends to
maximise individual responsibility. In a perfectly individualistic world, one
is never liable for damages. If one causes damage, others have failed to get
out of one's way. In a perfectly communalist world, one is always and already
liable for what one does.

> *Duncan Kennedy*: Hey, it's pitch-dark in here.

> *Author (interrupts typing)*: Sure, that's just the right setup for existential
> leaps in the dark!

> *Duncan Kennedy*: C'mon, gimme a break, I don't believe in this crap
> anymore!

Balkin explains that the two positions distinguished make sense only if they
are opposites. What matters, in other words, is the contrast. This contrast is
reflected at different levels of argumentation in the context of tort law.

At a very elementary level, for example, it is necessary to decide which
liability rule is to apply in which type of case, namely either strict liability or
liability that is based on fault. If the two are contrasted, the former appears to
be more communalist than the latter. If one adopts the individualistic variant
for a constellation of cases and thus considers fault-based liability to be the
appropriate standard, the question arises which standard of care ought to be
relevant for the determination of negligence. The question is whether reasonable care should be subjectively understood, ie with regard to the care that a
particular person is capable of exercising, or with regard to a typical 'ordinary'
person, which would imply a standard that anyone has to meet regardless
of whether it is too difficult for them. The first variant is individualistic, the
second is communalistic. If, to protect the injured party, one chooses an objective standard of care, then one chooses the communalist position. Hence,
after having chosen the more individualistic position in the first round, legal
knowledge then begins to pursue a 'zigzag course'. After individualism has
been affirmed in deeming fault-based liability appropriate, communalism
provides the background for selecting the standard of care. Possibly, at the next
juncture, the argument will swing back to the opposing position.

Balkin calls such switching the 'doctrinal conundrum'. The production of legal knowledge alternates between these positions without compelling reasons for choosing one over the other. Rather, the reasons are entirely redundant. The arguments for and against more or less individual responsibility recur at different levels of rule choices. Remarkably, owing to their stereotypical nature, they lack the power to persuade. Legal argumentation always runs on the same tracks. It is issued in writings to impress clients or to show off one's own skills vis-à-vis colleagues.

The alternation between these positions is unending. Once an objective standard of care has been chosen, it is conceivable to accommodate exceptions for certain groups of persons (minors or people with disabilities). Then the individualistic position comes to the fore again.

## § 166

From this general observation, Balkin draws three conclusions concerning legal knowledge.[14]

First, there are no compelling reasons why one position is chosen at one point and the other at another. Repeatedly, however, judges will feel compelled to move in either direction.

Second, because of this moment of necessitation the legal concepts turn out to harbour 'nested oppositions'. In each pole of an opposition the respective opposite has already taken root. If, for example, one wants to base contractual obligations exclusively on the declared will of the parties, one must be ready to admit at some point that there may be circumstances in which conduct must be counted as a declaration of will, even if the person has never formed a relevant intention.

Third, the negative system that Balkin reconstructs is hidden, as it were, within the positive system. The impression of coherence emphasised by Dworkin arises merely because moral consciousness is just as antinomic as legal thought. This is evident by looking at political ideologies. Conservatives are 'individualistic' in the economic sphere and 'communalist' when it comes to punishment and public safety. The zigzag course thus acquires a certain solidity at the level of ideology. It is therefore possible to predict court decisions reliably by focussing on ideology, possibly more reliably than by looking at the doctrines exhibited in judicial opinions.

[14] See also his 'Ideology', n 13.

§ 167

This disunity is telling. It says something about the state of practical reason. No argument can convince from the point of view of the counterargument. Conviction is something that people acquire or happen to have by chance.

Facing up to division, practical reason is, hence, confronted with a profound crisis of confidence. Argumentation at best amounts to some form of aggregation. Arguments are intellectually as numb as votes.

> *Child*: Yes or no.

> *Arnold Schönberg (moving a hand puppet of the Archangel Gabriel in his right hand)*: Whether right, left, forward or backward, uphill or downhill – you have to go on without asking what lies before or behind you.

Once we are faced with hard cases, we no longer know what is right. Any insistence that the right answer has been found seems as strange as an act of autohypnosis.

§ 168

With this experience in mind, another approach takes seriously the idea that, at the end of the day, legal reasoning is just as good or as bad as the counting of ballots.

The theory relevant in this context is the so-called 'Social Choice Theory'.[15] Among other things, it analyses the aggregation of individual decisions into group decisions. The phenomenon that immediately stands out in this context is the 'cycling' of results.

The phenomenon can be easily understood by looking at one standard example: Three candidates are running for political office, A, B and C. Voters D, E and F are invited to rank their preferences. This could look like this:

|   | A | B | C |
|---|---|---|---|
| D | 1 | 2 | 3 |
| E | 3 | 1 | 2 |
| F | 2 | 3 | 1 |

[15] See, for example, J Elster and A Hylland (eds), *Foundations of Social Choice Theory* (Cambridge, Cambridge University Press, 1986); JS Kelly, *Social Choice Theory: An Introduction* (Berlin: Springer, 1988).

If in a first round of voting A and B are on the ballot, then A will win for the reason that two voters, D and F, prefer A to B. If B and C are sent into the race, B will win, because D and E have a preference for B. If A and C face an election, then C wins, because E and F prefer C over A. The result is intransitive. It is not that A wins against C because he wins over B and B over C. Rather, the result is a cycle: A < B < A < C.

We end up with undecidability.

§ 169

Lewis Kornhauser and Larry Sager were among the first to bring Social Choice Theory to bear on the analysis of legal decision making.[16] The 'doctrinal paradox' that they present concerns different aggregation methods for rulings on multi-person judicial panels. Depending on whether one counts the votes on sub-issues or the final conclusion, the result can turn out quite differently.

Imagine the simple question of whether there is an obligation to pay damages depending on whether the defendant was at fault in engaging in unlawful conduct, and assume also that the question is decided by a panel of three judges:

|          | Illegality | Fault | Liability |
|----------|------------|-------|-----------|
| A        | Yes        | No    | No        |
| B        | No         | Yes   | No        |
| C        | Yes        | Yes   | Yes       |
| Majority | Yes        | Yes   | No/Yes    |

If what counts is how the majority decides on the sub-issues and if these decisions are therefore aggregated, liability must be affirmed. If one subjects the overall conclusion by the individual judges to a majority vote, then liability must be denied. The decision remains uncertain. But what is to be done?

Of course, one can engage in deep and long-winded controversies about which aggregation procedure would be the right one to pick.

---

[16] See LA Kornhauser and LG Sager, 'The One and the Many: Adjudication in Collegial Courts' (1993) 81 *California Law Review* 1–59.

§ 170

In the work of Leo Katz, the use of Social Choice Theory is nothing short of amazing. In his most recent book *Why the Law Is So Perverse*[17] he tries to explain why, if we follow the law, we are confronted with phenomena such as loopholes or the tormenting necessity to settle for one of two alternatives.

Katz has understood that legal theory is not legal super-science. It cannot remove the intellectual obstacles that may remain in the search for the right answer once doctrine has run its course. Rather, legal theory must explain where these obstacles stem from and why the production of legal knowledge remains an exasperating business.

The basic idea is simple. Several different criteria are usually relevant for an evaluation of legal questions. Heuristically, it is rewarding to imagine the criteria (or principles) to behave like voters who have preferences for certain outcomes.

In a situation of self-defence, the principle that nobody must take disproportionate measures against an attacker can be confronted with several options on which the principle will 'vote' as follows:

| Kill the attacker | Let the attacker kill you | Find a safe way out |
|---|---|---|
| No | Yes | Yes |

The principle votes yes and no. As long as there's a safe way out, one must not kill the attacker. The principle votes yes for the safe way out, for this is an option that it can approve of. Allowing oneself to be killed by an attacker is perhaps not the most appealing option, but it is consistent with taking no disproportionate measures. The principle, again, votes yes. However, killing an attacker right away, without knowing whether or not she is actually attempting a homicide, is an option to which the principle has to say no.

The basic idea is that principles show voting behaviour. Katz then observes how interpersonal aggregation paradoxes recur at the level of

---

[17] L Katz, *Why the Law Is So Perverse* (Chicago, IL, Chicago University Press, 2011). A predecessor work, with which he is no longer satisfied, is *Ill-Gotten Gains. Evasion, Blackmail, Fraud, and Kindred Puzzles of the Law* (Chicago, Chicago University Press, 1996).

intrapersonal cycles as indecisiveness. We begin with a consumer choice in order to demonstrate the parallel of the inter- and the intrapersonal:

|           | BWM | Mercedes | Audi |
|-----------|-----|----------|------|
| Franz     | 1   | 2        | 3    |
| Ferdinand | 3   | 1        | 2    |
| Felix     | 2   | 3        | 1    |

You get to the cycle by aggregating the preferences in pairs. BMW < Audi < Mercedes < BMW < Audi …. The same happens when people are replaced with criteria:

|        | BWM | Mercedes | Audi |
|--------|-----|----------|------|
| Power  | 1   | 2        | 3    |
| Safety | 3   | 1        | 2    |
| Beauty | 2   | 3        | 1    |

Such latent indecisiveness is suppressed in the practice of law. This explains why the law is so perverse.

> *The initiate, the pupil and the reader follow the author's Power Point presentation. Schönberg sits bent forward, his elbows resting on his thighs, and surrounds the back of the head with his hands. You cannot tell if he is covering his ears. The hand puppet of the Archangel Gabriel rises from the ground and says*: It must be hidden; you were permitted to see, but now you must forget it in order to fulfil the task.

## § 171

According to Katz, an analogous cycle can occur when one is confronted with a legal case in which several criteria or principles claim their relevance.

His prime example of this is a possible triage scenario. After an accident, two persons are injured, namely Al and Chloe. If Al does not receive treatment right away, there is a high risk that both of his legs are going to remain stiff. In the event of a treatment delay, Chloe, by contrast, would only have to put up with a slight impairment in the dexterity of her index finger. The principle according to which people are to be treated according to the severity of their injury would thus unquestionably accord priority to Al.

But Al loves Chloe and knows that she is a passionate piano player. Consequently, he decides to take a pass on his priority in favour of Chloe. The principle according to which people may voluntarily organise their affairs even if they thereby harm themselves permits him to do so.

However, already at this point we are not quite sure whether this principle is really applicable. Our hesitation suggests that we are possibly encountering a loophole here.

Now Bea comes into play. She is injured on one leg, which could also remain stiff if it is not treated right away. She is spoiling Al's generous sacrifice. She demands to be taken care of first because she is more seriously injured than Chloe.

Bea's intervention changes how we perceive the situation. So far, we have seen it through the lens of two principles: the severity of the injury, on the one hand, and the respect for choices and voluntary transactions, on the other. Confronted with the transfer of priority from Al to Bea, we react with amazement and without knowing why what Bea demands does indeed seem right to us.

> *Initiate*: Strange, but why not?
>
> *Pupil*: Someone donates his belongings to his heirs during his lifetime in order to save them the inheritance tax.
>
> *Initiate*: Strange, but why not?

With the appearance of Bea, the situation alters considerably. Suddenly, the chosen transfer of the priority of treatment appears to be frivolous. The loophole closes again. The relevance of the first principle is restored.

Owing to the restored relevance of the first principle, however, Al now takes precedence over Bea because of his comparatively more serious injury. Bea has nothing to complain about. Therefore, Al will again insist that he is free to transfer his right to priority of treatment to Chloe. We arrive at: Chloe < Bea < Al < Chloe ....

|  | Al | Bea | Chloe |
|---|---|---|---|
| Severity of the injury | 1 | 2 | 3 |
| Voluntary transfer | 2 | 3 | 1 |

The only way out of this predicament is to reject one principle as irrelevant. In this case, we are inclined to say that the principle of voluntary transfer has to give way. The right of treatment according to the severity of the injury thus becomes inalienable. It becomes as inalienable as human dignity, which prohibits people from selling themselves into slavery, even if it were useful to them, or prisoners from shortening their sentence by exchanging time for torture (an example discussed by Katz).

Katz does not mean to suggest that the glory of human dignity outdoes voluntary transaction objectively. He believes that the impression of the greater weight of this principle is ultimately explained by the need to prevent cycling. It would be more appropriate, actually, to allow the conflicting principles of our inherently divided practical reason to circulate.

The suppression of cycling is what makes the law perverse, and not the cycling itself.

## § 172

Katz has a very fine sense of how the presence or absence of certain facts can make the relevance of principles or criteria appear doubtful or excluded. A self-induced situation of self-defence can create a loophole in relation to the principle that an assailant does not forfeit his right to life as long as there is still a possibility of evading his attack.

| Kill the assailant in self-defence | Seek a safe way out |
| --- | --- |
| No | Yes |

But if a situation has arisen in which there is no safe way out, then this principle is suspended because it is no longer relevant. Then, all we are left with is:

| Kill the assailant in self-defence |
| --- |
| Yes |

A similar behaviour can be observed for foreigners who, through public criticism of the government of their home country, deliberately create a situation in which they would no longer be safe at home. It is thus given into their hands to make themselves eligible to be recognised as refugees.

They have the power to suspend the application of the principle according to which it is left to each state to determine the period of presence on its territory it grants to foreign residents.

## § 173

The list of riddles that Katz explores in his work is long. In addition to offering an analysis of why voluntary transfers are prohibited and how loopholes can be exploited, he seeks to clarify the binary nature of legal distinctions ('either-or') and the limits of criminal liability.

The result is that legal thinking is and always will be frustrating.

It is frustrating above all because practical reason – so long as it freely and informally can leave itself merely to reasoning – has no problem with moving in cycles between different solutions. In its divided state, in which it aggregates arguments, it is just as irresponsible as Freud's unconscious, which is, in his view, the medium for the articulations of the desires of the Id.

Internally divided practical reason does not arrive in the world of decision and action. For the law to reach a determinate state it must overcome this state and thus shed its natural tendency to indecisiveness.

Where It was, shall be I.[18] The path leading thereto is not a happy one. Freud was aware of that.

Katz's work is one of the most important contributions to elucidating the role of the unconscious in legal knowledge.

---

[18] S Freud, 'Neue Folge der Vorlesungen zur Einführung in die Psychoanalyse' in A Mitscherlich, A Richards and J Strachey (eds), *Studienausgabe*, vol 1 (Frankfurt aM, Fischer, 1982) 488–610, 516.

# The Legal Relation

## § 174

This chapter will answer all remaining questions.

    *Reader:* All?

    *Author:* All.

## § 175

If legal theory were a competitive race, American legal realism would emerge victorious from its history. With the demise of legal positivism and the divided shape of objective spirit, what remains for legal knowledge are merely the sobering insights that were first prepared by the realists. The beginning of the story of legal theory is also its end. Critical Legal Studies and Social Choice Theory root its ending only more deeply in the moral domain.

Thus, every person who tries to obtain guidance in and from law should be prepared to ask two questions: How are those to whom one is de facto subordinated likely to decide? How should they decide?

The second question is a question of morality. This does not change even if we do not know what the right answer is. According to legal realism, there is no obligation outside of morality.

And yet, the picture developed by the legal realists is incomplete. What they failed to elucidate is why their sobering insights are always treated like dirty little secrets that nobody must divulge in the official precincts of legal thought. We participate in the routines of legal knowledge by using an artificial normative language, which we nevertheless suspect of lacking any *direct* authority. Why is this the case? Why persist with this tenacious duality between the routines of legal thinking, on the one hand, and the purportedly really decisive factors, on the other?

Legal realism offers no other explanation than that people were formerly steeped in scholasticism and prejudice. The routines of legal thinking stem from the past that lingers. Despite the realistic interventions, however, this past does not cease to continue into the present. This suggests that the duality between the stage of legal knowledge and the real decisive factors is possibly part of what the law is.

§ 176

Modern legal positivism emphasised correctly that in the eyes of those who are seriously engaged in making legal claims the law appears to be composed of binding standards. This relevance of normativity is part of what explains the division between the shared project of interpreting legal norms and the function of interpretations to serve 'extra-legal' ends. Legally speaking, one communicates commitment, but only to others, not – or only rarely – to oneself.

> *Pupil*: The law requires that …

Those claiming to know what the law is assert what is objectively permitted or prescribed or prohibited or in some person's power. The speakers, however, raise their claims in pursuit of some strategy or an agenda or in the exercise of a certain role or capacity. Speaking legally is a means to an end. There would be no legal talk if such talk did not reap rewards on grounds external to the law, such as advancing the self-interest or affirming moral conviction.

In view of this dual commitment – that is, to legality and to any interest underlying invocations of the law – the question arises as to what it is that may actually limit the strategic use of the shared legal vocabulary. It would mark the touchstone designating the bindingness of the law.

When it comes to determining the strategically besieged legal normativity, the weakness of modern legal positivism emerges clearly enough. Legal positivism wants to distinguish the normativity of law from moral obligation. But how can we make sense of this difference without reducing the 'legal ought' to a mere must? Above all, the question must arise as to *whose* commitment we talk about once we sever the ties to the moral grounds of action. Whose volition is expressed in the law? And why do the attempts to remedy the internal weaknesses of legal positivism lead to various forms of rupture and division?

These are the unanswered questions of legal theory.

§ 177

> *Reader*: I would never have guessed that these are the remaining questions.
>
> *Author*: That is why you depend on my gentle guidance.
>
> *The reader smiles admiringly. The author blushes.*

## § 178

One comes closer to answering these questions when one understands the law as a relation between people.[1] It is a specific relation of making and justifying demands. Its function and meaning can be explained by examining more closely a reflexive form of moral universalisation.[2]

Only a few analytical steps need to be taken to traverse from ordinary moral judgement to the legal relation (see § 185).

## § 179

Universalisation is the form of moral judgement. On the ground of this form such a judgement asserts the generalisability of what is claimed. If it meets this condition, the judgement formulates a serious claim to validity.

> *Mother (to the child)*: You mustn't do that. No one must.

According to Kant, universalisation, in order to succeed, must first and foremost avoid internal contradiction.[3] Nobody can take out a loan with the intent not to repay it. Such an intent would immediately cross out the act of borrowing. One would get oneself some money, but one would not take out a loan.

In his view, universalisation also requires the absence of what he calls a contradiction in will. It arises, for example, when people rank the interests of others lower than their own and refuse to help those in need, while expecting support from others if they were in need themselves.

> *Poet*: My heart is cold and my soul is free. I never help anyone, and I am never in need of being helped myself. I walk through life and stand justified.

---

[1] The theory of the legal relation can be developed from various angles. A classical analysis of the relationship between rights and obligations is provided by WN Hohfeld, *Fundamental Legal Conceptions as Applied in Judicial Reasoning* (ed WW Cook, New Haven, CT, Yale University Press, 1946). Not exactly light fare – but highly worth reading – is the analysis of the distanced relationship between legal entities by Michael Oakeshott, 'The Rule of Law' in his *On History and Other Essays* (Indianapolis, IN, Liberty Fund, 1983) 129–78.

[2] For further thoughts developed in this chapter, see my work *The Legal Relation: Legal Theory after Legal Positivism* (Cambridge, Cambridge University Press, 2017).

[3] Immanuel Kant develops his ideas of universalisation in the *Groundwork of the Metaphysics of Morals* (ed J Timmerman, Cambridge, Cambridge University Press, 2009). On contradictions 'in conception' and contradictions 'in will', see O O'Neil, *Acting on Principle: An Essay in Kantian Ethics*, 2nd edn (Cambridge, Cambridge University Press, 2013) 26–27, 136–42.

## § 180

Both forms of 'contradiction' can be reconstructed from the perspective of a role change.[4] Universalisation is a way of looking at our own behaviour under conditions of reciprocity from the point of view of those who are likely to be affected by it. If everyone knows that I will not return the money I borrow, then I will not receive any. The behaviour collapses due to an 'internal contradiction'. If everyone knows that I am not ready to help, others are not going to help me. Obviously, universalisation rests on reciprocity. Even if much charitable work is done regardless of reciprocity, we would regard it as permissible for people to stop giving to people who are themselves not willing to help others even though they could. It is not morally wrong not to reward avarice.

Universalisation alone is not sufficient to resolve moral conflicts. An additional teleological element is required. It must be known in advance what purposes are to be realised in order to justify possible sacrifices or interference through an exchange of roles. We must already want property in order to disallow theft. Whether rules can be universalised depends on whether one can at least expect people to pursue certain goals. We must share at least a 'thin' theory of the good.

> *Initiate*: What is that supposed to mean?
>
> *Child*: The thin theory of the good was introduced by John Rawls in his *Theory of Justice* in order to arrive at an intersubjectively shared understanding of what we all want in spite of the fact that we may harbour different ideas about the good life. At the centre of the thin theory of the good is the idea that we mutually recognise our need for basic goods as 'all-purpose-means'. Basic goods are the goods needed for whatever else we may want to have or accomplish in our life.[5]

## § 181

Visions of the good life and the varieties of evaluative outlooks from which they are endorsed can conflict with one another. Most straightforwardly,

[4] On universalisation and role taking, see, first and foremost, GH Mead, *Mind, Self, and Society from the Standpoint of a Social Behaviorist* (ed C Morris, Chicago, IL, University of Chicago Press, 1934) and RM Hare, *Moral Thinking: Its Levels, Method, and Point* (Oxford, Oxford University Press, 1981).

[5] See J Rawls, *A Theory of Justice* (Cambridge, MA, Harvard University Press, 1971) 395–99.

such conflicts occur in the case of interferences with the freedom of others. How much noise does one have to endure? How much competition is unobjectionable? How much criticism do we have to take?

Those having deaf ears and a thick skin are not so affected by noisy or rough company. But not all are sound-insensitive pachyderms. Nor is there any good reason to expect these qualities from people. We cannot expect everyone to have them. A formally universalised moral judgement, which presupposes general noise insensitivity, would remain particular in its content. It may be agreeable to people of a certain character, ie the sound-insensitive pachyderms, but not to others. It depends on their evaluative outlook.

## § 182

Owing to the disagreements that reflect the actual diversity of evaluative outlooks, universalisation has to be raised to another level at which we can take on the task of universalising particular universalised content. In other words, it has to become reflective.

> *Initiate (in leather gear, gets off the motorcycle, takes off his helmet and says with a wink)*: Loud is good! *(He raises his right-hand thumb)*.

The motto of some motorcyclists which holds that loud engine noise is good can be universalised for the operation of engines during night-time hours under the condition that the population finds satisfaction in being aroused from sleep by the sound of a Harley Davidson. Even if real Harley fans might enjoy such a nightly confirmation of their lifestyle, universalisation requires that fans put themselves in the shoes of persons who need sleep and consider the sound of a motorcycle to be the mother of all insolence.

> *President Trump*: That's a disgrace! *(The author nods heftily)*.

Any mutual role change, however, would not lead beyond the point at which the characters merely confront one another. Harley Davidson fans would take themselves with them if they put themselves into the position of the persons desperately trying to get some sleep. The latter would hence be replaced by the former. It may therefore seem that, conversely, the Harley Davidson fans must equip themselves with the sensitivity of noise-affected persons for the purpose of universalisation. But the problem would persist even under this condition because now the Harley Davidson fans were the ones disappearing from the picture.

§ 183

It may be suggested that universalisation can only succeed by encouraging everyone, for the purpose of changing roles, to put themselves in the position of an ordinary person, whose attitudes would be located, as it were, in the middle between the two extremes.

> *Jones*: A little engine noise is okay, but please not too loud!

Harley Davidson fans and the noise-averse would thus have to accept what seems tolerable from the middling position envisaged by the ordinary person.

But that cannot solve the problem. For the difficulty that arises in the context of universalisation is that, from the point of view of each universalising person, this person *already* is the epitome of the ordinary person. Universalisation in and of itself insinuates ordinariness. The evaluative outlook of the person involves a positive or negative orientation towards goals that facilitates universalisation in the first place. Any outlook does, and any outlook is as good as any other.

> *Initiate*: How can the noise be disturbing when we are talking about a Harley? Don't be hysterical!
>
> *Author*: What's the point of such a disgraceful driving gig, while normal people want to get some sleep? *(President Trump nods approvingly, patting the author on the shoulder).*
>
> *Child (steps onto the ramp of the stage and speaks to the audience hiding her mouth towards the stage with one hand)*: Obviously, a hermeneutic gulf separates the initiate and the author. They attribute different weights to values. They consider different things to be relevant (see § 24).

§ 184

If it is not possible for the evaluative outlooks involved to merge into one – and taken as a given that no one must oust the other, for otherwise universalisation would fail – reciprocity can only be established by eliminating both. This means that universalisation can be successful on the condition that none of the outlooks involved partakes of it in a leading role. Rather, paradoxically speaking, both can only participate on the condition of being disregarded. The abstraction from evaluative outlooks must not, however, amount to reintroducing some ordinary person through the back door. Otherwise, the judgement would still be tainted with particularity. The ordinary person's outlook is merely one among others (see § 183).

As the evaluative outlook is pushed into the background, a transformation occurs. Thus,

> *Initiate*: Loud engine noise is good because everyone must realise that it's cool.

is transformed into

> *Initiate*: I want loud engine noise.

The corresponding rejection of the noisy nuisance for the (let's face it, compelling) reason that it represents the mother of all insolence is turned into:

> *Author*: I do not want to hear that noise.

With that the problem changes. The claim to validity of a moral judgement is transformed into an act of will and thus rendered as a choice. Since in the medium of intersubjective reciprocity the legitimacy of willing cannot be derivative of what certain people consider to be their good, it can only be based on respect for choices. The claim to validity of the act of will is still debatable. What matters now, however, is not which evaluative outlook underpins a particular will but the conditions under which certain acts of will are *generally* acceptable.

The key question becomes, then, whether and to what extent freedom of choice must be respected.

## § 185

Reflective universalisation marks the origin of the legal relation. Practical reason can thus have practical impact by wearing 'will' and 'choices' as its social face.

In the direct relation between persons with divergent evaluative outlooks, the moral judgement of one appears to be plainly wrong from the perspective of the other.

> *Initiate (to the author)*: Stuffy old prick!
>
> *Author (to the initiate)*: Ruthless buffoon, shame on you!
>
> *President Trump (to no one in particular)*: You are a disgrace!

Reciprocity can only be sustained by disregarding content. The judgement of the other must nevertheless be respected at the reflexive level so long as it satisfies the formal requirement of universalisation, which now means that it has to be consistent with universalisation for acts of will.

Still, the universalisation for acts of will could still remain self-serving when it asserts in the guise of a liberty the activity that one wishes to engage in pursuant to one's own outlook.

> *Initiate*: Everyone should be free to ride a motorcycle at night.

This is insufficient to bracket the outlook. In order to permit many conceivable outlooks, the liberty has to be formulated at a level of greater generality.

> *Initiate*: Anyone should be free to drive around so long as there is no harm done to others.

### § 186

Those with different outlooks encounter in judgements of others their own reasons in a different form (see § 23). These judgements can only be accepted if the social and substantive dimensions of moral judgement part company.

> *Substantive dimension*: Your judgement is wrong.

> *Social dimension*: I respect your judgement because it would be wrong to assume that I am a more prudent or morally better person than you are.

If, for the purpose of reciprocal recognition, the moral judgement is substantively reduced to an act of will, it also loses access to what warrants it and what accounts for its soundness.

Remarkably, then, practical reason, in order to realise itself, must absorb its partial negation. Respect is to be shown for what is merely an act of will and not for the reasons making the will intelligible. But this respect is nonetheless necessary, for otherwise nobody could ever safely earn respect for what he or she believes to have reason to do.

The will of others is indeed accepted. Substantively, however, it is *unwillingly* accepted.

> *Child (shaking her head)*: Yes, go forward, but don't expect me to understand you.

The background of such partial self-negation, which allows practical reason to become a reality, is the divide between the substantive and the social dimensions of moral judgement. This antinomy can be resolved with regard to what remains after one has bracketed the evaluative dimension of judgement. What remains is choice along the social dimension, ie within an 'external' relation to others.

## § 187

Any line-drawing of spheres of volition depends, however, on practical reason. There is no way to wash out all particularity. The evaluative outlooks must be bracketed even though they sustain their practical relevance. This may seem like squaring the circle

Paying respect along the social dimension takes place against the ever present possibilities of substantive *isosthenia* – the tie between reasons – or a complete mutual lack of understanding.

> *Initiate (to the author)*: Stuffy old prick!

> *Author (to the initiate)*: Ruthless buffoon, shame on you!

> *President Trump*: C'mon guys, give it a break now.

Indeed, the possibility of practical reason remains overshadowed by its own impossibility. The demarcation of freedom of choice must be prepared for conflicting moral judgements. This is the reason why any moral line drawing must be carried out in the form of a decision.

Decisions are an expression of second-order morality. They legitimately set action free from the paralysis that besets it when it is tied down by insufficient reasons. At the level of intersubjective reciprocity, the reasons associated with particular evaluative outlooks are insufficient to establish common ground. Any resolution that favours one over the other can emancipate itself from the strictures of particularity only by severing the connection. Decisions signal the bracketing of the substantive dimension of moral judgement.

But bracketing means bracketing. The substantive dimension never disappears. It is never irrelevant. But the relevance changes. Questions of moral substance have to be recast as questions of power and competence.

> *Pupil*: Landlords should not terminate leases unless they need a dwelling themselves.

*Initiate*: Should the legislature have the power to proscribe such acts?

*Pupil*: What is the difference?

*Initiate*: The question is taken out of the moral domain into a sphere where we encounter pluralism and difference of opinion.

## § 188

*Moralist*: Nihilist!

*Nihilist*: Moralist!

## § 189

Practical reason can become real by resolving its antinomy within the legal relation.

A decision determines something. But it has to be implemented. In the case of law, the enforcement may involve coercion.

## § 190

People often conceive of the relation between law and coercion as somehow external. Legal norms are taken to be substantively so important that their observance cannot be left to chance, the accidental good will of people, or social pressure. Hence, any breach has to be fortified with harsh consequences.[6]

The threat of sanctions forces people to obey the law. Coercion affects the will. If the will is unimpressed by the content of a legal norm itself, then the threat of coercion is followed by an unyielding act of force that effectively conquers the will.

It all ends in violence.

> *(The pupil, the mother, the child and the legal realist cheer enthusiastically and slap each other mutually on their raised palms [they are doing a 'high five' in American parlance]).*

---

[6] This view of the relation between law and coercion is forcefully criticised by Christoph Kletzer in his 'The Germ of Law' in C Bezemek, M Potacs and A Somek (eds), *Vienna Lectures on Legal Philosophy*, vol 1 (Oxford, Hart Publishing, 2018) 1–20.

## § 191

This view is not implausible. It does not do justice, however, to the fact that the obligation that arises with the legal relation is an expression of unwilling volition. Whoever accepts, out of respect for the judgement of others and subject to social reciprocity, the choices of others is 'willing' those choices unwillingly. This gives us the form of legal validity.

Unwillingness is also volition that is subject to coercion. Not all unwilling willing is. But it will be seen that unwillingly willing what others want in the medium of the legal relation is *compatible* with being coerced into wanting it.

## § 192

When one is acting out of insight, one also wants what one does. Acting is then based on a free choice. Insofar as choice reflects insight it is not arbitrary. When matters are at stake into which people have put their hearts, the absence of arbitrariness rises to the level of necessity. Once they endorse something overwhelmingly, they experience what they choose as something that they cannot but want.

## § 193

Necessitation felt as a result of insight is different from coercion. Nevertheless, on the surface they may look alike.

In situations of coercion or existential plight, persons are confronted with choices they would rather not make. This is the case for two reasons.

First, existential plight or coercive threats confront persons with having to choose between (at least) two evils. If it were not for this inescapable choice, they would not be interested in any of the options.

Second, it is nonetheless immediately clear what the choice must be. For a father, the choice between paying ransom and losing his daughter's life is not really a choice. He must pay ransom. He has to do it because of who he is, namely a father (see § 192).

## § 194

The identity of the choosing person, which becomes salient in this situation, predetermines the choice. It functions as a norm that does not admit of any exception.

Through a coercive act, the identity-constituting attitudes of persons are used as means to make them want something that they would not want if it were not for the coercive situation. They can be made to want the lesser evil because they cannot avoid having to choose between at least two, one of which is disproportionately greater than the other.

Coercion makes persons want what they would not want on their own. Their will is loath, but also determined. They are willing unwillingly.

## § 195

Acting from insight also involves one's personal identity. It does not, however, as though one is possessed of one's identity as if this were the consequence of a curse. The identity is shaped in a biographical process in which persons construct and reconstruct their normative orientations in interchange with individual actions. Identity remains in flux because the persons are challenged and seduced by tempting options, which to adopt, can alter, at least slightly, who they are.

This playful process of variation is foreclosed by a forced choice between two evils. A specific part of the conglomerate of voluntarily assumed roles whose loose interaction constitutes personal identity is affected by the threat. This part is engaged by the impending evil and thus pulled to the centre of the personality where it dominates everything. The father of a kidnapped daughter is just a father. A man threatened by an armed robber is merely a frightened creature.

The elusive whole that constitutes persons beyond their roles or functions disappears. This whole that remains inaccessible to any final determination – particularly since it is constantly renewed in the course of action – becomes subordinated to one of its parts.

## § 196

The inevitability of a choice between two evils is not the only irritating aspect of coercion. The forced persons retain powers of volition. They therefore commit themselves to something. Coercion affects the will but does not destroy it. Once persons are exposed to coercive threats, they know what they have to do. Compulsion produces a reason for action.

Thus understood, coercion is, surprisingly perhaps, a source of obligations. The obligation originates, however, from that part of the person whose dominance is triggered by the threat. What disappears of the persons, hence, is what they are over and above their parts. It is ousted by that part of the persons to which the coercive threat is directed. Not only do the persons have no choice but to want what they must want, it is wanted *for them* by what is only part of their self. This invariable dominance of the part over the whole explains why coercion offends autonomy.

If the coercive situation is purposefully brought forward by another person, then the unavoidable will of the coerced persons becomes an instrument to attain the goals of the other. The will of the compelled persons is caused by the will of the offender because they would not ever have wanted what they now want if it had not been for the threat. Unwilling volition is heteronomous.

There is no moral obligation to realise the evil preferred in a situation of coercion outside of this situation (within the situation the obligation incessantly flickers between 'on' and 'off'). The coercive situation is a substitute for the lack of moral obligation. Coercion is a substitute for authority, which is lacking.

Each form of coercion reveals a binding force that does not originate from moral insight. It always raises the question of whether a lack of real authority is de facto compensated for or whether a precaution is taken against the unreasonableness of the addressees.

## § 197

*Child (cranky)*: No! No-o!

*Mother*: You'll do that right now. That's reasonable. You'll do that now. That's reasonable. You'll do that now, or it'll hurt.

*Reader (to the author)*: Your examples are conspicuously misogynistic.

*Father*: You'll do that right now. That's reasonable. You'll do that now. That's reasonable. You'll do that now, or it'll hurt.

*Author (to the reader)*: Better?

*Reader (to the author)*: Yes.

## § 198

Unwilling volition is the form of legal validity and a fortiori of legal obligation. It is by no means external to the law to be given effect by coercive threats. Coercion and legal validity share the same volitional structure.

At the level of the legal relationship, nobody has to understand, let alone agree with, what other persons want. As to the alleged sublimity of motorcycle noise, the persons exposed to the noise may remain unimpressed. We cannot and must not expect them to tolerate this sound on the ground of admitting that there is something good about it.

> *Initiate (almost roaring to the author)*: Don't be so stubborn! You must understand that!

The obligation to accept what others do cannot and need not be based on accepting their reasons for action. But since there has to be an obligation, for otherwise reciprocity would collapse, it is only possible to ground it in the substitute authority of coercion.

Coercion can create an obligation where in the relation between persons good reasons are of no avail. Legal demands by others and norms imposed by lawgivers have no substantive moral authority. They are unwillingly accepted owing to the prevalence of the social dimension of moral judgement. Given that this is their form of validity it is permissible to use coercion as a substitute for substantive authority. Otherwise, the edifice of practical reason would collapse.

## § 199

However, in order to arrive at a proper understanding of legal obligation, Austin's conception must be turned upside down (see § 89 and § 94). Legal obligation does not arise from coercion. Rather, in order for the legal relation to be possible, there must be an obligation that is not based on accepting the choices of others on moral terms. Coercion is capable of generating an obligation of this kind. Since the obligation must be *real* and *effective*, there may be coercion.

Yet, the relationship between law and coercion is even closer.

Ultimately, the divergence of moral judgement confronts us with a predicament. We are faced with the undesirable alternative of either having to give room to the will of others, even if we think it is wrong, as in the case of the nightly operation of a motorcycle, or losing access to the realisation of our own freedom, which is only possible on the basis of that reciprocity which enables us to appear in the social world as judging and acting beings. Since we want to be free acting beings, losing reciprocity would be more severe than yielding to the otherness of others and the associated encounter with our altered reason (see § 23). The circumstances of human life force us to choose the legal relationship. Our social nature compels us to do so. We have no choice but to be the beings that we are.

There is nothing illegitimate about being forced by the human condition. Likewise, there is nothing wrong with using coercion to realise the legal relation.

There is a limit, however, to the endorsement of reciprocity. It would undermine itself if it resulted in a world in which we could no longer position ourselves. The theory of the legal relation cannot do without the concept of evil. Evil is different from what is merely immoral. It shakes our confidence in the world.[7]

## § 200

> *Reader*: Please come to the end. I'm tired, and it all seems very philo-
> sophical to me.
>
> *Author*: As you wish.

## § 201

The bindingness of the law differs from the bindingness of morality. The root of the difference is reflective universalisation. The law arises when morality differentiates itself from itself and gives rise to something else.

The validity of law is based on decisions. They symbolise detachment from any particular evaluative outlook. In this respect, legal validity is the moral obligation of no one in particular. Put differently, it is what becomes of our moral obligation once we have left the domain of ordinary moral judgement.

The legal obligation reflects unwilling volition, that is, the substantively unwilling acceptance of what others choose (see § 198). In order to give life to this form of volition, the law uses coercive threats. Coercion is the way of articulating the significance of the social dimension of moral judgement.

---

[7] The view that the experience of evil shatters our trust in the world is developed by S Neiman, *Evil in Modern Thought: An Alternative History of Philosophy* (Princeton, NJ, Princeton University Press, 2002).

Whoever wills unwillingly distances themself from what they nonetheless endorse. All affirmation always involves also a disclaimer, every assertion is also a revocation.

Legality is the social face of irony.

## § 202

Coercion observes the structure of reasons for action created by law. The authority, however, of what the law says is owed to decisions. All law originates from sources. It does not exhaust itself in what is de facto enforced. Enforcement requires lending force to valid laws.

Legal knowledge, narrowly understood (see § 31), is tailored to determine what someone may demand from others. In order to fit this outlook, it has to arrive at constructive interpretations of the sources. Such interpretations have to pay heed to the principle inherent in the legal relation, which is the equal treatment of equals. The systematic elaborations of the law that originates from sources is taking its cue from equality. This is the source of the limits that are drawn to strategic uses of legal arguments (see § 176).

## § 203

The bindingness of legal validity is adequately expressed in the legality of conduct. One observes the law externally, ie without consideration of the reasons which make the law appear substantively reasonable. In law – in the demands of others or in the impositions on the part of the legislature – we encounter the claims of 'altered' reason (see § 23).

Legality is also decisive for understanding what the appropriate attitude is for the pursuit of legal knowledge. The attitude of willing unwillingly what originates from altered reason is best captured in the jaunty irony with which detached legal scholarship elaborates what ought to be done.

The adequate attitude of legal knowledge is best grasped by comparing it with the hermeneutic effort of those engaged in interpreting the works of an important author (see already § 38). Such an interpretation will indeed strive to give the work the best possible appearance in light of the intentions attributable to the author. However, the interpretation will always be subject to the proviso that the truth or falsity of the work is irrelevant to the appropriateness of the interpretive enterprise. It is conceivable to develop revealing interpretations of works, even if as an interpreter one ultimately comes to the conclusion that they are quite absurd.

The emancipation from the burden of having to defend the work against potential critics invests interpretations with playful grace. Thinking rises boldly above the responsibility for what is thought by elaborating the thoughts of an author who is likely long dead and thus cannot object to the interpretation of his or her thinking.[8]

In the case of legal knowledge, this serenity is revealed in the gusto with which what is claimed is apologetically attributed to the law or to legally constituted authority.

> *Initiate*: Human dignity prohibits shooting down an airplane that has been hijacked by terrorists who are intent on letting it crash over a densely populated area. The passengers killed would be degraded to mere means by such a firing and thus not respected as ends in themselves. This is, at any rate, how the jurisprudence of the Federal Constitutional Court can be understood.

Because of the emancipation from responsibility for the reasonableness of law, the irony of legal knowledge sometimes takes on a Romantic colouring.[9] Then its proper domain appears to be the game of arguments and counterarguments. Some philosophers of the Romantic period perceive in the dialogical process – in which thought is immediately trailed by its counterthought – a variety of irony. Thought would thus end up in an infinite circle of creation and destruction, in which nothing is fixed. Legal knowledge, which is – as in the case of moot court training – produced in simulations and not forced to yield a decision, easily grows into such a Romantic format. Every decision seems intellectually impoverished compared to the subtlety with which arguments and counterarguments could be rolled out perpetually.

No matter how one approaches it, from the point of view of those who argue and anxiously anticipate counterarguments or from the perspective of

---

[8] What I claim about the serene irony of interpreters of great works is correct only if Brandom is right that we can distinguish *de dicto* from *de re* interpretations. See RB Brandom, *Tales of the Mighty Dead. Historical Essays in the Metaphysics of Intentionality* (Cambridge, MA, Harvard University Press, 2002) 99–102. This view has been challenged by C Lafont, 'Meaning and Interpretation: Can Brandomian Scorekeepers be Gadamerian Hermeneuts?' (2007) 2 *Philosophy Compass* 1–13.

[9] On the irony of the Romantics, see E Behler, *Klassische Ironie – Romantische Ironie – Tragische Ironie: Zum Ursprung dieser Begriffe* (Darmstadt, Wissenschaftliche Buchgesellschaft, 1972).

deciders who are aware of the vulnerability of their arguments, the production of legal knowledge remains a frustrating business.

§ 204

The reason for the duality left unexplained by the realists (see § 175) is finally apparent. The legal knowledge works with attributions of validity, albeit with an ironic deflection that is appropriate for dealing with altered reason.

The use of this knowledge must stand trial before the tribunals of self-interest and morality. Nevertheless, it has its own weight in the face of our moral vernacular. This weight stems from its efforts to work through the legal materials constructively. In the spirit of Dworkin's 'scheme' (see § 149), the point of all efforts at elaboration is like treatment of like cases.

The ruptures and divisions we encounter in legal thinking are descendants of the antinomy of practical reason. It is always possible to arrive at different decisions.

§ 205

*The poet enters the stage in the middle of which is placed a narrow table. On the table sits a tape recorder. The poet presses the 'Play' button. One hears the voice of the convict*: You Nazi swine!

*The light goes out, the curtain falls quickly.*

# Bibliography

## 1. Recommended Introductory Works

BH Bix's magisterial *Jurisprudence: Theory and Context*, 8th edn (Durham, NC, Carolina Academic Press, 2019) provides an excellent introduction to legal theory. It offers a comprehensive overview of the major currents and occasionally some more detailed examinations of various issues. Outstanding also are NE Simmonds, *Central Issues in Jurisprudence: Justice, Law and Rights*, 4th edn (London, Thomson, 2013) and R Wacks, *Understanding Jurisprudence: An Introduction to Legal Theory*, 5th edn (Oxford, Oxford University Press, 2017). See also L Murphy, *What Makes Law: An Introduction to the Philosophy of Law* (Cambridge, Cambridge University Press, 2014).

Very useful reference works are D Patterson (ed), *A Companion to Philosophy of Law and Legal Theory*, 2nd edn (Oxford, Wiley-Blackwell, 2010) and BH Bix, *A Dictionary of Legal Theory* (Oxford, Oxford University Press, 2004) and J. Coleman and S Shapiro (eds), *The Oxford Handbook of Jurisprudence and Philosophy of Law* (Oxford, Oxford University Press, 2004).

For an anthology of important texts of the Anglo-American tradition, see D Patterson (ed), *Philosophy of Law and Legal Theory* (Oxford, Oxford University Press, 2003).

An introduction to newer continental European approaches can be found in S Buckel, R Christensen and A Fischer-Lescano (eds), *Neuere Theorien des Rechts*, 3rd edn (Tübingen, Mohr, 2020).

## 2. Works Cited

Alexander, GS, 'Comparing the Two Legal Realisms – American and Scandinavian' (2002) 50 *American Journal of Comparative Law* 131–74.

Alexy, R, *A Theory of Constitutional Rights* (trans J Rivers, New York, Oxford University Press, 2002).

—— *A Theory of Legal Argumentation: The Theory of Rational Discourse as Theory of Legal Justification* (trans R Adler and N MacCormick, Oxford, Oxford University Press, 1989).

—— *Mauerschützen: Zum Verhältnis von Recht, Moral und Strafbarkeit* (Göttingen, Vandenhoeck & Ruprecht, 1997).

—— *The Argument from Injustice: A Reply to Legal Positivism* (trans B Litschewski Paulson and SL Paulson, Oxford, Oxford University Press, 2010).

Arendt, H, *Lectures on Kant's Political Philosophy* (ed Ronald Beiner, Chicago, IL, University of Chicago Press, 1999).

Augsberg, I, *Die Lesbarkeit des Rechts. Texttheoretische Lektionen für eine postmoderne juristische Methodologie* (Weilerswist, Velbrück, 2009).

Augustine, *On the Trinity: Books 8–15* (trans S McKenna, Cambridge, Cambridge University Press, 2002).

Austin, J, *The Province of Jurisprudence Determined* (ed W Rumble, Cambridge, Cambridge University Press, 1995).

Austin, JL, *How to Do Things With Words* (Cambridge, MA, Harvard University Press, 1962).

Balkin, J, 'Deconstructive Practice and Legal Theory' (1987) 96 *Yale Law Journal* 743–86.

—— 'Taking Ideology Seriously: Ronald Dworkin and the CLS Critique' (1987) 55 *University of Missouri Kansas City Law Review* 392–433.

—— 'The Crystalline Structure of Legal Thought' (1986) 39 *Rutgers Law Review* 1–110.

Behler, E, *Klassische Ironie – Romantische Ironie – Tragische Ironie: Zum Ursprung dieser Begriffe* (Darmstadt, Wissenschaftliche Buchgesellschaft, 1972).

Bergbohm, K, *Jurisprudenz und Rechtsphilosophie*, vol 1 (Leipzig, Duncker & Humblot, 1892).

Berman, HJ, *Law and Revolution: The Formation of the Western Legal Tradition* (Cambridge, MA, Harvard University Press, 1983).

Bix, B, *Law, Language and Legal Determinacy* (Oxford, Clarendon Press, 1993).

Bjarup, J, 'The Philosophy of Scandinavian Legal Realism' (2005) 18 *Ratio Juris* 1–15.

Brandom, RB, *Making it Explicit: Reasoning, Representing, and Discursive Commitment* (Cambridge, MA, Harvard University Press, 1994).

—— *Tales of the Mighty Dead. Historical Essays in the Metaphysics of Intentionality* (Cambridge, MA, Harvard University Press, 2002).

Bratman, M, *Acting Together: A Planning Theory of Agency* (Oxford, Oxford University Press, 2014).

Broderick, A (ed), *The French Institutionalists: Maurice Hauriou, Georges Renard, Joseph T. Delos* (trans M Welling, Cambridge, MA, Harvard University Press, 1970).

Burton, SJ, *The Path of the Law and Its Influence: The Legacy of Oliver Wendell Holmes, Jr.* (Cambridge, Cambridge University Press, 2000).

Chang, R, *Incommensurability, Incomparability, and Practical Reason* (Cambridge, MA, Harvard University Press, 1997).

Chaouli, M, *Thinking with Kant's Critique of Judgment* (Cambridge, MA, Harvard University Press, 2017).

Cohen, FS, *Ethical Systems and Legal Ideals: An Essay on the Foundation of Legal Criticism* (New York, Falcon Press, 1933).

—— 'Transcendental Nonsense and the Functional Approach' (1935) 35 *Columbia Law Review* 809–49.

Cohen, LD (ed), *The Legal Conscience: Selected Papers of Felix S. Cohen* (New Haven, CT, Yale University Press, 1960).

Coleman, J (ed), *Hart's Postscript. Essays on the Postscript to the Concept of Law* (Oxford, Oxford University Press, 2001).

—— 'Negative and Positive Positivism' (1982) *Journal of Legal Studies* 139–64.

—— *The Practice of Principle: In Defence of a Pragmatist Approach to Legal Theory* (Oxford, Oxford University Press, 2001).

Coleman, J and Shapiro, S (eds), *The Oxford Handbook of Jurisprudence and Philosophy of Law* (Oxford, Oxford University Press, 2002).

Cook, WW, 'The Logical and Legal Bases of the Conflict of Laws' (1924) 33 *Yale Law Journal* 457–88.

De Wilde, M, 'The Dark Side of Constitutionalism: Carl Schmitt Reading Santi Romano' (2018) 11 *Ethics & Global Politics* 12–24.

Derrida, J, *Limited Inc* (trans S Weber, Evanston, IL, Northwestern University Press, 1988).

Duarte de Almeida, L, Edwards, J and Dolcetti, A (eds), *Reading HLA Hart's The Concept of Law* (Oxford, Hart Publishing, 2013).

Duxbury, N, *Patterns of American Jurisprudence* (Oxford, Oxford University Press, 1995).

—— 'Robert Hale and the Economy of Legal Force' (1990) 53 *Modern Law Review* 421–44.

Dworkin, R, *Justice for Hedgehogs* (Cambridge, MA, Harvard University Press, 2013).

—— *Law's Empire* (Cambridge, MA, Harvard University Press, 1986).

—— *Taking Rights Seriously*, 2nd edn (Cambridge, MA, Harvard University Press, 1978).

Ehrlich, E, *Die juristische Logik*, 2nd edn (Tübingen, Mohr, 1925).

Elster, J and Hylland, A (eds), *Foundations of Social Choice Theory* (Cambridge, Cambridge University Press, 1986).

Falk, U, *Ein Gelehrter wie Windscheid: Erkundungen auf dem Gebiet der sogenannten Begriffsjurisprudenz* (Frankfurt aM, Klostermann, 1989).

Finnis, J, *Natural Law and Natural Rights* (Oxford, Clarendon Press, 1980).

Fish, SL, *Doing What Comes Naturally* (Oxford, Oxford University Press, 1989).

—— *There's No Such Thing as Free Speech* (New York and Oxford, Oxford University Press, 1994).

Fisher III, W, Horwitz, M and Reed, TA, *American Legal Realism* (New York, Oxford University Press, 1993).

Förster, E, *The Twenty-Five Years of Philosophy: A Systematic Reconstruction* (trans B Bowman, Cambridge, MA, Harvard University Press, 2012).

Forster, P, *Peirce and the Threat of Nominalism* (Cambridge, Cambridge University Press, 2011).

Frank, J, *Law and the Modern Mind* (New York, Brentano's, 1930).

Frege, G, *Logical Investigations* (trans PT Geach and RH Stoothoff, New Haven, CT, Yale University Press, 1977).

Freud, S, 'Neue Folge der Vorlesungen zur Einführung in die Psychoanalyse' in A Mitscherlich, A Richards and J Strachey (eds), *Studienausgabe*, vol 1 (Frankfurt aM, Fischer, 1982) 488–610.

Fried, BH, *The Progressive Assault on Laissez Faire: Robert Hale and the First Law and Economics Movement* (Cambridge, MA, Harvard University Press, 1998).

Fuller, LL, *The Morality of Law* (New Haven, CT, Yale University Press, 1969).

Gabriel, M, *Transcendental Ontology: Essays on German Idealism* (New York, Continuum, 2011).

Gardner, J, *Law as a Leap of Faith: Essays on Law in General* (Oxford, Oxford University Press, 2012).

'Gnaeus Flavius', 'Der Kampf um die Rechtswissenschaft' (1906), in T Würtenberger (ed), *Rechtswissenschaft und Soziologie* (Karlsruhe, C.F. Müller, 1962) 13–40.

Gostomzyk, T and Viellechner, L (eds), *Denken in Netzwerken: Zur Rechts- und Gesellschaftstheorie von Karl-Heinz Ladeur* (Tübingen, Mohr, 2009).

Gray, CB, *The Methodology of Maurice Hauriou: Legal, Sociological, Philosophical* (Amsterdam, Rodopi, 2010).

Green, MS, 'Legal Realism as a Theory of Law' (2005) 46 *William and Mary Law Review* 1915–2000.

Grey, TC, 'Langdell's Orthodoxy' (1983) 45 *University of Pittsburgh Law Review* 1–53, reprinted in S Brewer (ed), *The Philosophy of Legal Reasoning: A Collection of Essays by Philosophers and Legal Scholars* (London, Routledge, 1998) 115–67.

Guest, S, *Ronald Dworkin*, 3rd edn (Stanford, CA, Stanford University Press, 2012).

Günther, K, *The Sense of Appropriateness: Application Discourses in Morality and Law* (trans J Farrell, Albany, NY, State University of New York Press, 1993).

Häberle, P, *Die Wesensgehaltsgarantie des Art. 19 Abs. 2 des Grundgesetzes*, 3rd edn (Heidelberg, C.F. Müller, 1983).

Habermas, J, *Diskursethik*, Philosophische Texte vol 3, 4th edn (Berlin, Suhrkamp, 2019).

Hale, RL, *'Bargaining, Duress, and Economic Liberty'* (1943) 43 *Columbia Law Review* 603–28.

—— 'Coercion and Distribution in a Supposedly Non-Coercive State' (1923) 38 *Political Science Quarterly* 470–94.

Hare, RM, *Moral Thinking: Its Levels, Method, and Point* (Oxford, Oxford University Press, 1981).

Hart, HLA, 'Positivism and the Separation of Law and Morals' (1958) 71 *Harvard Law Review* 593–621.

—— *The Concept of Law*, 2nd edn (Oxford, Clarendon Press, 1994).

Hauriou, M, *Tradition in Social Science* (trans CB Gray, Amsterdam, Rodopi, 2011).

Haverkamp, HP, *Georg Friedrich Puchta und die 'Begriffsjurisprudenz'* (Frankfurt aM, Klostermann, 2004).

Heck, P, *Das Problem der Rechtsgewinnung – Gesetzesauslegung und Interessenjurisprudenz – Begriffsbildung und Interessenjurisprudenz* (ed R Dubischar, Bad Homburg vor der Höhe, VAS Verlag, 1968).

Henkel, T, *Begriffsjurisprudenz und Billigkeit: Zum Rechtsformalismus der Pandektistik nach G. F. Puchta* (Cologne, Böhlau, 2004).

Herget, JE and Wallace, S, 'The German Free Law Movement as the Source of American Legal Realism' (1987) 73 *Virginia Law Review* 399–455.

Hershovitz, S (ed), *Exploring Law's Empire, The Jurisprudence of Ronald Dworkin* (Oxford, Oxford University Press, 2006).

—— 'Wittgenstein on Rules: The Phantom Menace' (2002) 22 *Oxford Journal of Legal Studies* 619–40.

Himma, KE, *The Nature of Law: Philosophical Issues in Conceptual Jurisprudence and Legal Theory* (New York, Foundation Press, 2011).

Hobbes, T, *Leviathan* (ed I Shapiro, New Haven, CT, Yale University Press, 2010).

Hohfeld, WN, *Fundamental Legal Conceptions as Applied in Judicial Reasoning* (ed WW Cook, New Haven, CT, Yale University Press, 1946).

Holmes, OW, 'The Path of the Law' (1897) 10 Harvard Law Review 457–78.

Hookway, C, *The Pragmatic Maxim: Essays on Peirce and Pragmatism* (Oxford, Oxford University Press, 2012).

Houlgate, S, *The Opening of Hegel's Logic: From Being to Infinity* (West Lafayette, Purdue University Press, 2006).

Hutchinson, AC, *Critical Legal Studies* (Totowa, NJ, Rowman and Littlefield, 1988).

Jhering, R, *Der Geist des römischen Rechts auf den verschiedenen Stufen seines Entwicklung*, vol 1, 6th edn (Leipzig, Breitkopf und Härtel, 1907); vol 2/2, 5th edn (Leipzig, Breitkopf und Härtel, 1898).

Kalman, L, *Legal Realism at Yale, 1927–1960* (Chapel Hill, NC, University of North Carolina Press, 1986).

Kant, I, *Critique of Pure Reason* (trans P Guyer and A Wood, Cambridge, Cambridge University Press, 1998).

—— *Critique of the Power of Judgment* (trans P Guyer and E Matthews, Cambridge, Cambridge University Press, 2000).

—— *Die Metaphysik der Sitten*, Werkausgabe vol 8 (ed W Weischedel, Frankfurt aM, Insel, 1968).

—— *Groundwork of the Metaphysics of Morals* (ed J Timmerman, Cambridge, Cambridge University Press, 2009).

—— *Kritik der Urteilskraft* (ed H Klemme, Hamburg, Meiner, 2009).

—— *Lectures on Logic* (ed and trans JM Young, Cambridge, Cambridge University Press, 1992.

—— *The Metaphysics of Morals* (trans M Gregor, Cambridge, Cambridge University Press, 2017).

Kantorowicz, HU, 'Some Rationalism about Realism' (1934) 43 *Yale Law Journal* 1240–53.

Katz, L, *Ill-Gotten Gains. Evasion, Blackmail, Fraud, and Kindred Puzzles of the Law* (Chicago, IL, Chicago University Press, 1996).

—— *Why the Law Is So Perverse* (Chicago, IL, Chicago University Press, 2011).

Kelly, JS, *Social Choice Theory: An Introduction* (Berlin: Springer, 1988).

Kelman, M, *A Guide to Critical Legal Studies* (Cambridge, MA, Harvard University Press, 1988).

Kelsen, H, *Allgemeine Staatslehre* (originally published 1925, ed M Jestaedt, Tübingen, Mohr, 2019).

—— *Allgemeine Theorie der Normen* (Vienna, Manz, 1979, published posthumously by R Walter and K Ringhofer).

—— *Das Problem der Souveränität und die Theorie des Völkerrechts: Beitrag zu einer reinen Rechtslehre* (Tübingen, Mohr, 1920).

—— *Der soziologische und der juristische Staatsbegriff: Kritische Untersuchungen des Verhältnisses von Staat und Recht* (Tübingen, Mohr, 1922).

—— *General Theory of Law and State* (originally published 1945, ed AJ Treviño, London, Routledge, 2005).

—— *General Theory of Norms* (trans M Hartney, Oxford, Clarendon Press, 1991).

—— *Hauptprobleme der Staatsrechtslehre entwickelt aus der Lehre vom Rechtssatz, Werke* vol 2.1 (ed M Jestaedt, Tübingen, Mohr Siebeck, 2008).

—— *Introduction to the Problems of Legal Theory* (trans B Litschewski Paulson and SL Paulson, Oxford, Clarendon Press, 1992).

—— *Pure Theory of Law*, 2nd edn (trans M Knight, Berkeley, CA, University of California Press, 1967).

—— 'Rechtswissenschaft und Recht: Erledigung eines Versuchs zur Überwindung der "Rechtsdogmatik"' (1922) in SL Paulson (ed), *Die Rolle des Neukantianismus in der Reinen Rechtslehre: Eine Debatte zwischen Sander und Kelsen* (Aalen, Scientia, 1988)

—— *Reine Rechtslehre* (Leipzig, Deuticke 1934, and 2nd edn Vienna, Deuticke, 1960).

—— *Reine Rechtslehre* (ed M Jestaedt, Tübingen, Mohr, 2008).

—— *Über Grenzen zwischen juristischer und soziologischer Methode* (Tübingen, Mohr, 1911).

Kennedy, D, *A Critique of Adjudication. Fin de Siecle*, Cambridge, MA, Harvard University Press, 1997).

—— 'Form and Substance in Private Law Adjudication' (1976) 89 *Harvard Law Review* 1685–778.

—— *Legal Reasoning: Collected Essays* (Aurora, Davies Group Publishers, 2008).

—— 'The Structure of Blackstone's Commentaries' (1979) 28 *Buffalo Law Review* 205–382.

Klatt, M (ed), *Institutionalized Reason: The Jurisprudence of Robert Alexy* (Oxford, Oxford University Press, 2012).

Kletzer, C, 'Absolute Positivism' (2013) 42 *Netherlands Journal of Legal Philosophy* 87–99.

—— 'The Germ of Law' in C Bezemek, M Potacs and A Somek (eds), *Vienna Lectures on Legal Philosophy*, vol 1 (Oxford, Hart Publishing, 2018) 1–21.

—— *The Idea of a Pure Theory of Law* (Oxford, Hart Publishing, 2018).

Korb, AJ, *Kelsens Kritiker: Ein Beitrag zur Geschichte der Rechts- und Staatstheorie (1911–1934)* (Tübingen, Mohr, 2010).

Kornhauser, LA and Sager, LG, 'The One and the Many: Adjudication in Collegial Courts' (1993) 81 *California Law Review* 1–59.

Korsgaard, CM, *Self-Constitution: Action, Identity, and Integrity* (Oxford, Oxford University Press, 2009).

Kramer, M, *In Defence of Legal Positivism: Law without Trimmings* (Oxford, Oxford University Press, 1999).

Krawietz, W (ed), *Theorie und Technik der Begriffsjurisprudenz* (Darmstadt, Wissenschaftliche Buchgesellschaft, 1976).

Kripke, SR, *Wittgenstein on Rules and Private Language: An Elementary Exposition* (Cambridge, MA, Harvard University Press, 1982).

Ladeur, KH, *Die Textualität des Rechts. Zur poststrukturalistischen Kritik des Rechts* (Weilerswist, Velbrück Verlag, 2005).

—— *Postmoderne Rechtstheorie: Selbstreferenz – Selbstorganisation – Prozeduralisierung* (Berlin, Duncker & Humblot, 1995).

Lafont, C, 'Meaning and Interpretation: Can Brandomian Scorekeepers be Gadamerian Hermeneuts?' (2007) 2 *Philosophy Compass* 1–13.

LaTorre, M, *Law as Institution* (Dordrecht, Springer, 2010).

Leiter, B, *Naturalizing Jurisprudence: Essays on American Legal Realism and Naturalism in Legal Philosophy* (Oxford, Oxford University Press, 2007).

Llewellyn, K, *The Bramble Bush: On our Law and Its Study*, 11th edn (New York, Oxford University Press, 2008).

Luhmann, N, *A Sociological Theory of Law* (trans E King and M Albrow, London, Routledge and Kegan Paul, 1985).

—— 'Die Einheit des Rechtssystems' (1983) 14 *Rechtstheorie* 129–54.

—— *Law as a Social System* (trans A Ziegert, Oxford, Oxford University Press, 2004).

—— *Legitimation durch Verfahren*, 4th edn (Frankfurt aM, Suhrkamp, 1986).

MacCormick, N and Weinberger, O, *An Institutional Theory of Law* (Dordrecht, Reidel, 1986).

Marmor, A, *Interpretation and Legal Theory* (Oxford, Clarendon Press, 1992).

—— *Philosophy of Law* (Princeton, NJ, Princeton University Press, 2011).

Marx, K and Engels, F, *Manifesto of the Communist Party* (London, William Reeves, 1988)

—— and —— *Werke*, vol 4 (Berlin, Dietz Verlag, 1977).

Mead, GH, *Mind, Self, and Society from the Standpoint of a Social Behaviorist* (ed C Morris, Chicago, IL, University of Chicago Press, 1934).

Mecke, CE, *Begriff und System des Rechts bei Georg Friedrich Puchta* (Göttingen, V & R unipress, 2009).

Menke, C, *Tragic Play: Irony and Theater from Sophocles to Beckett* (trans J Phillips, New York, Columbia University Press, 2009).

—— *Tragödie im Sittlichen: Recht und Gerechtigkeit nach Hegel* (Frankfurt aM, Suhrkamp, 1996).

Merkl, AJ, *Die Lehre von der Rechtskraft entwickelt aus dem Rechtsbegriff: Eine rechtstheoretische Untersuchung* (Leipzig and Vienna, Deuticke, 1923).

Müller, F and Christensen, R, *Juristische Methodik, Grundlegung für die Arbeitsmethoden der Rechtspraxis*, vol 1, 11th edn (Berlin, Duncker & Humblot, 2013).

Neiman, S, *Evil in Modern Thought: An Alternative History of Philosophy* (Princeton, NJ, Princeton University Press, 2002).

Nietzsche, F, *On the Genealogy of Morality*, 3rd edn (trans C Diethe, Cambridge, Cambridge University Press, 2017).

—— *The Gay Science* (trans J Naukhoff, Cambridge, Cambridge University Press, 2001).

O'Neil, O, *Acting on Principle: An Essay in Kantian Ethics*, 2nd edn (Cambridge, Cambridge University Press, 2013).

Oakeshott, M, 'On History and Other Essays (Indianapolis, IN, Liberty Fund, 1983).

Olechowski, T, *Hans Kelsen: Biographie eines Rechtswissenschaftlers* (Tübingen, Mohr, 2020).

Patterson, D, *Law and Truth* (New York, Oxford University Press, 1996).

Pauer-Studer, H, *Justifying Injustice: Legal Theory in Nazi Germany* (Cambridge, Cambridge University Press, 2020).

Pauer-Studer, H and Fink, J (eds), *Rechtfertigungen des Unrechts: Das Rechtsdenken des Nationalsozialismus in Originaltexten* (Berlin, Suhrkamp, 2014).

Paulson, SL, 'Arriving at a Defensible Periodization of Hans Kelsen's Legal Theory' (1999) 19 *Oxford Journal of Legal Studies* 351–64.

—— (ed), *Die Rolle des Neukantianismus in der Reinen Rechtslehre: Eine Debatte zwischen Sander und Kelsen* (Aalen, Scientia, 1988).

—— 'The Basic Norm Revisited' in L Duarte de Almeida, J Gardner and L Green (eds), *Kelsen Revisited: New Essays on the Pure Theory of Law* (Oxford, Oxford University Press, 2013) 42–61.

—— 'The Neo-Kantian Dimension of Kelsen's Pure Theory of Law' (1992) 12 *Oxford Journal of Legal Studies* 311–32.

Pavlakos, G (ed), *Law, Rights and Discourse: The Legal Philosophy of Robert Alexy* (Oxford, Hart Publishing, 2007).

—— *Our Knowledge of the Law: Objectivity and Practice in Legal Theory* (Oxford, Hart Publishing, 2007).

Peirce, CS, 'How to Make Our Ideas Clear', reprinted in M Cohen (ed), *Chance, Love, and Logic* (New York, Harcourt, Brace and Company, 1923) 32–60.

Pihlajamäki, H, 'Against Metaphysics in Law: The Historical Background of American and Scandinavian Legal Realism Compared' (2004) 52 *American Journal of Comparative Law* 469–87.

Pinkard, T, *Hegel's Phenomenology: The Sociality of Reason* (Cambridge, Cambridge University Press, 1994).

Pippin, RB, *Hegel's Practical Philosophy: Rational Agency as Ethical Life* (Cambridge, Cambridge University Press, 2008).

Popper, KR, 'Epistemology Without a Knowing Subject' (1968) 52 *Studies in the Logic and Foundations of Mathematics* 333–73.

Postema, GJ, *Bentham and the Common Law Tradition* (Oxford, Clarendon Press, 1986).

Preuß, UK, *Die Internalisierung des Subjekts: Zur Kritik und Funktionsweise des subjektiven Rechts* (Frankfurt aM, Suhrkamp, 1979).

Puchta, GF, *Das Gewohnheitsrecht*, vol 1 (Erlangen, Palmsche Verlagsbuchhandlung, 1828); vol 2 (Erlangen, Palmsche Verlagsbuchhandlung, 1837).

Radbruch, G, 'Legislative Injustice and Supra-Statutory Law' (1946), trans B Litschewski Paulson and SL Paulson, (2006) 26 *Oxford Journal of Legal Studies* 1–11.

—— *Rechtsphilosophie: Studienausgabe*, 2nd edn (ed R Dreier and SL Paulson, Heidelberg, C.F. Müller, 2003).

Rawls, J, *A Theory of Justice* (Cambridge, MA, Harvard University Press, 1971).

Raz, J, *Between Authority and Interpretation: On the Theory of Law and Practical Reason* (Oxford, Oxford University Press, 2009).

—— *Ethics in the Public Domain: Essays in the Morality of Law and Politics*, 2nd edn (Oxford, Oxford University Press, 1995).

—— *Practical Reasons and Norms*, 3rd edn (Oxford, Oxford University Press, 1999).

—— *The Morality of Freedom* (Oxford, Clarendon Press, 1986).

Rickert, H, 'Vom Begriff der Philosophie' (1910) 1 *Logos* 1–34.

Riebschläger, K, *Die Freirechtsbewegung: Zur Entwicklung einer soziologischen Rechtsschule* (Berlin, Duncker & Humblot, 1969).

Ripstein, A (ed), *Ronald Dworkin* (Cambridge, Cambridge University Press, 2007).

Romano, S, *The Legal Order* (trans M Croce, Abingdon, Routledge, 2017).

Rumble, WE, *American Legal Realism* (Ithaca, NY, Cornell University Press, 1968).

Rundle, K, *Forms Liberate: Reclaiming the Jurisprudence of Lon L. Fuller* (Oxford, Hart Publishing, 2013).

Rüthers, B, *Institutionelles Rechtsdenken im Wandel der Verfassungsepochen* (Berlin, Gehlen, 1970).

Sander, F, 'Die transzendentale Methode der Rechtsphilosophie und der Begriff der Rechtserfahrung' (1920) in SL Paulson (ed), *Die Rolle des Neukantianismus in der Reinen Rechtslehre: Eine Debatte zwischen Sander und Kelsen* (Aalen, Scientia, 1988) 75–114.

Saussure, F de, *Course in General Linguistics* (trans R Harris, London, Bloomsbury, 2013).

Schauer, F, 'Formalism' (1988) 97 *Yale Law Journal* 509–48.

—— *Thinking like a Lawyer* (Cambridge, MA, Harvard University Press, 2009).

Schlag, P, '"Le Hors de Texte, C'est Moi". The Politics of Form and the Domestication of Deconstruction' (1990) 11 *Cardozo Law Review* 1631–74.

—— 'The Problem of the Subject' (1991) 69 *Texas Law Review* 1627–743.

Schlegel, JH, 'American Legal Realism and Empirical Social Science: The Singular Case of Underhill Moore' (1980) 29 *Buffalo Law Review* 195–324.

Schmitt, C, *Constitutional Theory* (trans J Seitzer, Durham, NC, Duke University Press, 2008).

—— *Legality and Legitimacy* (trans J Seitzer, Durham, NC, Duke University Press, 2004).

—— *On the Three Types of Juristic Thought* (trans J Bendersky, Westport, CT, Praeger, 2004).

—— *Über die drei Arten des Rechtswissenschaftlichen Denkens* (Hamburg, Hanseatische Verlagsanstalt, 1934).

Schnädelbach, H, *Philosophy in Germany 1831–1933* (Cambridge, Cambridge University Press, 1983).

Searle, JR, *Speech Acts: An Essay in the Philosophy of Language* (London, Cambridge University Press, 1969).

Shapiro, I, *The Moral Foundations of Politics* (New Haven, CT, Yale University Press, 2003).

Shapiro, SJ, *Legality* (Cambridge, MA, Harvard University Press, 2013).

Silberg, S, *Hermann Ulrich Kantorowicz und die Freirechtsbewegung* (Berlin, Logos Verlag, 2005).

Simmonds, N, *Law as a Moral Idea* (Oxford, Oxford University Press, 2007).

Singer, JW, 'Legal Realism Now' (1988) 76 *California Law Review* 467–544.

Somek, A, *Der Gegenstand der Rechtserkenntnis: Epitaph eines juristischen Problems* (Baden-Baden, Nomos, 1996).

—— 'Legal Formality and Freedom of Choice: A Moral Perspective on Jhering's Constructivism' (2002) 15 *Ratio Juris* 52–62.

—— *Rechtliches Wissen* (Frankfurt aM, Suhrkamp, 2006).

—— *Rechtssystem und Republik: Über die politische Funktion des systematischen Rechtsdenkens* (Vienna, Springer, 1992).

—— *The Legal Relation: Legal Theory After Legal Positivism* (Cambridge, Cambridge University Press, 2017).

—— *Wissen des Rechts* (Tübingen, Mohr, 2018).

Spaak, T, *A Critical Appraisal of Karl Olivecrona's Legal Philosophy* (Berlin, Springer, 2014).

Summers, RS, *Instrumentalism and American Legal Theory* (Ithaca, NY, Cornell University Press, 1982).

Tamanaha, BZ, *A Realistic Theory of Law* (Cambridge, Cambridge University Press, 2017.

Teubner, G, *Constitutional Fragments* (Oxford, Oxford University Press, 2012).

—— *Law as an Autopoietic System* (Oxford, Basil Blackwell, 1989).

Theunissen, M, *Der Andere: Studien zur Sozialontologie der Gegenwart*, 2nd edn (Berlin, de Gruyter, 1977).

Tsuk Mitchell, D, *Architect of Justice: Felix S. Cohen and the Founding of American Legal Pluralism* (Ithaca, NY, Cornell University Press, 2007).

Tuori, K, *Ratio and Voluntas: The Tension Between Reason and Will in the Law* (Farnham, Ashgate, 2011).

Tushnet, M, 'Critical Legal Studies: A Political History' (1991) 100 *Yale Law Journal* 1515–44.

Twining, W, *Karl Llewellyn and the Realist Movement* (London, Weidenfeld & Nicolson, 1973, reprint 1985).

Underhill Moore, W and Callahan, CC, 'Law and Learning Theory: A Study in Legal Control' (1943) 53 *Yale Law Journal* 1–136.

Unger, RM, *False Necessity: Anti-Necessitarian Social Theory in the Service of Radical Democracy* (Cambridge, Cambridge University Press, 1988).

—— *Knowledge and Politics* (New York, Free Press, 1975).

—— *Passion: An Essay on Personality* (New York, Free Press, 1984).

—— *The Critical Legal Studies Movement* (Cambridge, MA, Harvard University Press, 1986), 2nd edn with the subtitle *Another Time, A Greater Task* (London, Verso, 2015).

von Jhering, R, *Der Geist des römischen Rechts auf die verschiedenen Stufen seiner Entwicklung*, vol 1, 6th edn (Leipzig, Breitkopf und Härtel, 1907); vol 2/2, 5th edn (Leipzig, Breitkopf und Härtel, 1898).

von Savigny, FC, *On the Vocation of Our Time for Legislation and Jurisprudence* (trans AH Abraham, London, Littlewood, 1831).

Waldron, J, *Law and Disagreement* (Oxford, Oxford University Press, 1999).

Walther, M, 'Hat der juristische Positivismus die deutschen Juristen im "Dritten Reich" wehrlos gemacht?' in R Dreier and W Sellert (eds), *Recht und Justiz im 'Dritten Reich'* (Frankfurt aM, Suhrkamp, 1989).

Waluchow, W, 'Legal positivism, inclusive versus exclusive' in *Routledge Encyclopedia of Philosophy*, www.rep.routledge.com/articles/thematic/legal-positivism-inclusive-versus-exclusive/v-1/sections/inclusive-and-exclusive-positivism.

Wieacker, F, *A History of Private Law in Europe* (trans T Weir, Oxford, Oxford University Press, 1995).

Wiethölter, R, *Rechtswissenschaft* (Frankfurt aM, Fischer, 1968).

Wilk, K, *The Legal Philosophies of Lask, Radbruch, and Dabin* (ed EW Patterson, trans K Wilk, Cambridge, MA, Harvard University Press, 1950).

Wittgenstein, L, *Philosophical Investigations*, 3rd edn (trans GEM Anscombe, Oxford, Blackwell, 2001).

Zaremby, J, *Legal Realism and American Law* (New York, Bloomsbury, 2014).

# Index

Lightning Source UK Ltd.
Milton Keynes UK
UKHW020419081221
395228UK00003B/34

9 781509 951291